MW00398827

SECRET
DELAWARE

A Guide to the Weird, Wonderful, and Obscure

Rachel Kipp & Dan Shortridge

Copyright © 2022, Reedy Press, LLC
All rights reserved.

Reedy Press
PO Box 5131
St. Louis, MO 63139
www.reedypress.com

No part of this publication may be reproduced or transmitted in any form or by any means, electronic or mechanical, including photocopy, recording, or any information storage and retrieval system, without permission in writing from the publisher. Permissions may be sought directly from Reedy Press at the above mailing address or via our website at www.reedypress.com.

Library of Congress Control Number: 2021950835
ISBN: 9781681063645

Design by Jill Halpin

Unless otherwise indicated, all photos are courtesy of the author or in the public domain.

We (the publisher and the author) have done our best to provide the most accurate information available when this book was completed. However, we make no warranty, guarantee, or promise about the accuracy, completeness, or currency of the information provided, and we expressly disclaim all warranties, express or implied. Please note that attractions, company names, addresses, websites, and phone numbers are subject to change or closure, and this is outside of our control. We are not responsible for any loss, damage, injury, or inconvenience that may occur due to the use of this book. When exploring new destinations, please do your homework before you go. You are responsible for your own safety and health when using this book.

Printed in the United States of America
22 23 24 25 26   5 4 3 2 1

Dedicated to the journalists—
the writers of the first draft of history.

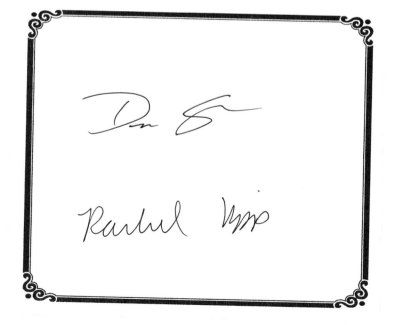

Fort Delaware
Credit: Delaware State Parks.

CONTENTS

ACKNOWLEDGMENTS

Delaware's history is long and rich, and near-impossible to condense into 85 short tales. We owe a huge debt of gratitude to Delaware's storytellers, historians, interpreters, state officials, educators, tourism leaders, journalists, and many more.

Our former colleagues in journalism unknowingly provided the background or inspiration for many of these stories. We especially want to thank robin brown, Patricia Talorico, and the late Molly Murray. Their knowledge and expertise of Delaware's people, places, and history, reflected in their decades of reporting, was especially invaluable.

A special thanks for their assistance in research and photography is due to Jessica Borcky, Gary Camp, Joe Capaldi, Captain Bones Bait and Tackle, Ed Kee, James Fisher, Christopher Heckscher, Stacey Hofmann, Nikki Lavoie, Hanna Manninen, Shauna McVey, Jason Minto, Dawn Mitchell, Mark Nardone, the New Jersey Department of Environmental Protection, John Petersen, Warren Rosenfeld, Thomas Summers, W. L. Gore & Associates, Jim Yurasek, and the staff of the Delaware Public Archives.

Above all, we want to thank our family, especially our kids, for putting up with our strange visits to out-of-the-way locations, our pauses on walks to take snapshots at odd places, and our incomprehensible conversations, like "Did you get a photo of the lima bean bag?" To Dassi, Matty, and Liam: thank you.

INTRODUCTION

There's a famous scene in the movie *Wayne's World* with a punchline rooted in the idea that Delaware doesn't have any memorable stories. But if you spend enough time here, you'll find that the First State is chock-full of quirky and unique tales— including one about Wayne and Garth.

This book profiles Delaware's best-kept secrets. As we set out to do our research, we found that many of them were hiding in plain sight—there were places that we'd visited and walked or driven past for years, but had never had the chance to really learn about. For example, we'd been to the sculpture garden at the Delaware Art Museum dozens of times, but never knew that one of its most iconic works of art was actually a dry run for a 9/11 memorial.

Rachel spent her first years in Delaware living blocks away from the famed studio of an iconic American illustrator, while Dan spent weekends as a teenager camping in a state park that has been home to a former quarantine station for immigrants, gun emplacements and bunkers designed to defend the East Coast against the Nazis, and—maybe—the burial spot of Captain Kidd's famed treasure. There were also a few stories that had been more carefully tucked away: using decades-old newspaper clippings, we found the true story behind an old well that promises eternal life to anyone who takes a sip, and the day-by-day news on how Seaford became the Nylon Capital of the World during the Great Depression.

When we wrote *100 Things to Do in Delaware Before You Die* a few years ago, it was with the goal of showing that often, there's no better place to go exploring than the place where you live. With *Secret Delaware*, we hope that we've given natives and newcomers alike even more reasons to love the First State and appreciate its history and stories.

—Rachel and Dan

THE ART OF ARDEN

How did an obscure economic idea create an artists' colony?

Arden is one of the most interesting places in Delaware. Look in the dictionary under "quaint," and you'll find a photo of its handful of streets lined with trees, sculptures, and whimsical painted objects.

"We've heard Arden is made up of hippies, of communists, of nudists, and there might be some precedent for a lot of those things, but we're not as crazy as it seems," remarked Lisa Themal Mullinax, editor of local publication the *Arden Page*.

Arden's unique roots stem from the ideas of Henry George, a thinker and economist arguing to just tax land and not property placed on it—the so-called "single-tax movement."

Followers Frank Stephens and Will Price created Arden in 1900, with all the underlying land on its 0.3 square miles held by a trust. Residents get a 99-year lease upon which to build their homes, sheds, gardens, and sculptures. At its height, George's ideas led to the creation of 17 similar single-tax communities around the country.

One early resident was muckraking journalist Upton Sinclair. In 1911, he and 11 others were arrested for playing baseball, allegedly breaking a 1793 law barring "gaming on the Sabbath." Charges were dropped after they spent a night in jail.

Other notable residents have included Ella Reeve Bloor, a labor organizer and political candidate, and President Joe Biden, for a time during his childhood.

THE ART OF ARDEN

WHAT: The Village of Arden

WHERE: 2119 The Highway, Arden, DE

COST: n/a

PRO TIP: Come for the atmosphere, stay for a show organized by the Concert Gild.

2

An outdoor amphitheater is home to plays and performances. Photos by Dan Shortridge

The Gild Hall is Arden's hub for concerts, events, and meetings.

Arden is now home to about 430 people. There are groups, or "Gilds," who sing, play instruments, and perform Shakespeare. The single-tax idea is just a governing tool rather than a main attraction for its residents, who love the arts-colony atmosphere and strong sense of community.

"It's 99 percent the art, the ambiance, as well as the aesthetics," says resident Mike Curtis.

The neighboring communities of Ardentown and Ardencroft are often grouped together as "the Ardens."

MITCHUM'S MARKER

Why is there a grave marker for Hollywood star Robert Mitchum in Delaware?

In the Odd Fellows Cemetery in Camden, people paying their respects to friends and family may stumble upon a small marker rising a few inches above the ground: "ROBERT CHARLES MITCHUM."

Yes, that's the same Robert Mitchum of Hollywood fame, star of movies and TV shows such as *Cape Fear, The Longest Day, and The Winds of War*.

What is he doing buried in Camden, Delaware?

Well, he's not. The marker there is a cenotaph, a monument honoring someone whose remains are located elsewhere. Mitchum's ashes were scattered at sea.

It turns out that the famous actor lived in Delaware for a time as a youth—and his wife hailed from here as well.

In the 1920s, Mitchum moved here with his newly widowed mother to live on his grandparents' farm near Felton.

As a teenager, he traveled cross-country living a vagabond life.

It was on a return visit to Delaware years later that he met future wife Dorothy Mitchum. Dorothy had been dating Mitchum's younger brother, John. The two were married "in the cabbage-scented kitchen of a Methodist parson in Dover," her obituary recalled. The couple lived in California and on the Eastern Shore of Maryland.

ROBERT MITCHUM'S CENOTAPH

WHAT: A marker for the late actor Robert Mitchum

WHERE: Odd Fellows Cemetery, 35 Rising Sun Rd., Camden, DE

COST: Free

PRO TIP: Bring a camera for a photo rather than tools to do a stone rubbing, which can damage headstones.

Actor Robert Mitchum is remembered with a marker at a Delaware cemetery in the same county where he lived for a time as a young man, next to one for his wife, Dorothy. Photo by Dan Shortridge

After Mitchum's death in 1997, his ashes were scattered off the California coast from a boat owned by friend and fellow actor Fess Parker. The marker was later put up in the Camden cemetery, along with one for Dorothy, who died in 2014.

Mitchum was known for his carousing and womanizing. When he once was asked for his life story, he reportedly replied: "What do you mean my life story? I told it all to the Los Angeles Police Department."

JOURNEY TO FREEDOM

What role did Delaware play in the Underground Railroad?

A Northern state with some Southern sensibilities, including the abhorrent slave trade, Delaware was well-positioned geographically to play an important role in the Underground Railroad.

The most prominent stationmaster helping Blacks escape to freedom in the North was Thomas Garrett, a white iron merchant. Garrett is said to have aided more than 2,500 fugitives from slavery; making it to Garrett's house was said to be as safe as stepping across the border to Canada. He was eventually charged in federal court in 1848, convicted, and fined several thousand dollars.

Another conductor was Samuel D. Burris, born a free Black man near Dover. He helped lead several people out of Maryland and Delaware to the North. Like Garrett, Burris was eventually also charged and convicted—only he was ordered to be sold into slavery as punishment. Thankfully, his "buyer" was Isaac Flint, an abolitionist from Wilmington, and Burris was soon returned to his family.

South of Dover, the tiny enclave of Magnolia was the chosen home for a large community of free Blacks, including many formerly enslaved people. These included several people

---

There are few written records about Delaware's involvement in the chain of aid that stretched from slave states to free states. Some locations were only mentioned using codes; many were identified in contemporary times thanks to stories passed down through generations.

Star Hill AME Church, near Magnolia, was built around 1866 by a community of Black residents including several Underground Railroad conductors. Photo by Rachel Kipp

JOURNEY TO FREEDOM

WHAT: Star Hill African Methodist Episcopal Church

WHERE: 357 Voshell Mill-Star Hill Rd., Dover, DE

COST: n/a

PRO TIP: Travel the complete Harriet Tubman Underground Railroad Byway, including to Tubman's home just over the border in Maryland: harriettubmanbyway.org.

who participated in the Underground Railroad. In 1863, they formed the Star Hill African Methodist Episcopal Church—the name representing the star that served as a guiding point for men, women, and children escaping from bondage.

To the north, a stop in the town of Odessa also provided refuge. On one occasion in the 1840s, an escapee known as Sam visited the home of Quakers Daniel and Mary Corbit, also abolitionists. Mary Corbit hid Sam in an attic cubbyhole, and he was not captured by a pursuing posse. The Corbits gave Sam money and food for the remainder of his journey. Their home today is known as the Corbit-Sharp House.

Though born in Maryland, Harriet Tubman also played a role in Delaware's pathway to freedom, primarily working with Garrett.

SPACE SUIT-UP

How did this company pave the way for humanity to walk on the moon?

In the 1960s, a division of the Playtex company landed a contract that would change the course of human and interstellar history.

ILC Industries, known at the time for manufacturing bras and girdles, was chosen by the United States government to create the suits that would protect the Apollo astronauts.

"ILC was a true underdog in the competition to provide the spacesuits," recalled historian and former ILC employee Bill Ayrey, author of a book about the company and the Apollo suits. "They were competing against major aerospace companies in the race to suit our astronauts for lunar survival."

Key to landing the deal was a prototype suit and a video ILC produced showing how easy it was to walk in it, recalled former ILC president Homer Reihm, then the chief project engineer. "NASA saw that video, and it was over," Reihm said. "At that point, the contract was ours."

It was heady times for a company founded as the International Latex Corporation in 1932 (thus "ILC").

Ayrey said while engineers designed the suits, it was the team of ILC seamstresses who played a critical role in their assembly.

"It was the ladies sitting at their Singer sewing machines that had to help the engineers figure out how to put it all together," he said. "They were the true heroes. If their work

---

ILC Dover's suits have been worn by NASA astronauts on six moon landings and 250 spaceflights, as well as more than 3,000 spacewalk hours. No suit has ever failed.

Right to left, astronauts Neil Armstrong, Michael Collins, and Buzz Aldrin, followed by ILC Dover technicians Joe Schmidt and Ron Woods, prepare for a countdown test in July 1969. Photo courtesy of NASA

resulted in a seam failure, an astronaut could lose their life."

Today, as ILC Dover, the company continues to work for NASA and other sensitive, highly precise government projects, such as creating components of suits to be used for exploring planets, floating in space, and traveling to the stars.

SPACE-SUIT-UP

WHAT: Historic marker at the former site of the International Latex Corporation, later ILC Dover

WHERE: 350 Pear St., Dover, DE

COST: n/a

PRO TIP: ILC's operations have since been moved to near Frederica, Delaware. The historic marker is at the location that's now the Campus Community School.

BIG BIBLE

Why is the governor sworn in on a 500-year-old Bible?

In 1532, the explorer Francisco Pizarro landed in Peru, Thomas More stepped down as Henry VIII's chancellor in England, and Suleiman the Magnificent began the second Ottoman invasion of Hungary.

Meanwhile, in Paris, a printer named Robert Stephens produced a Bible—a heavy, thick book written in Latin—which, nearly 500 years later, would play a key part in the civic ritual of Delaware.

The precise origins of Delaware's official state Bible are shrouded in mystery. It's not clear when the tome itself crossed the Atlantic or came to the First State, though it is believed that the book was a gift from France to Delaware. For what, or when, we do not know.

What is known is that the book has been used in the inauguration of nearly every governor of the state since Kent County Democrat William Tharp in 1847. The lone exception was in 1901, when Governor-elect John Hunn, a Quaker, opted to simply hold his hand high. "The old Latin Bible will miss the kiss of the only governor who has ever neglected it," the Wilmington newspaper wrote at the time in somewhat melodramatic fashion.

THE DELAWARE "STATE BIBLE"

WHAT: The Bible used at every governor's inauguration (except one) since 1847

WHERE: Seen and used at every inauguration, secured between events. The next chances to see it in public will be in January 2025 and January 2029.

COST: n/a

PRO TIP: Delaware's inaugurations are typically held outdoors, but these days you may get a better view and have a warmer seat by watching on a livestream at delaware.gov.

Left: *Gov. Walter Bacon is sworn in on the official state Bible in the 1940s. Photo courtesy of the Delaware Public Archives*

Right: *The state Bible is seen at Gov. John Carney's second-term inauguration in January 2021. Photo courtesy of the State of Delaware*

Inset: *The state Bible, written in Latin, was printed by Robert Stephens in the 1500s. Photo courtesy of the Delaware Public Archives*

Even then, the book was kept under close watch, stored in a fireproof case in the state library. By the 1970s, a reporter noted, it was only brought out for the inauguration and sometimes for special events. The book today is stored in the Delaware Public Archives under tight control.

In 2001, Delaware's first female governor, Ruth Ann Minner (see Pioneer Politician, page 162), was inaugurated using two Bibles—the 1532 Latin volume and her personal Bible given to her by a Sunday School teacher in 1949.

WAR AND THE WALL

Where can you see an artifact from the War of 1812 lodged in the side of a building?

More than 200 years ago, British ships sat off Delaware's Atlantic coast and lobbed artillery at the obstinate Americans. Today, just minutes from that same sea, a round black ball sits where it has been since that day in April 1813—embedded in the foundation of a Lewes home.

The Cannonball House, as it is known, sits on Front Street in Lewes and serves as a local museum of maritime history. The black iron cannonball fired from King George III's ships is a stark reminder of the War of 1812.

Built between 1765 and 1790, the Cannonball House is a simple house shingled in cypress. The house was owned in the 1800s first by a Methodist minister and then a ship pilot. The building has been a restaurant and magistrate's office, among other uses.

During the War of 1812—which actually lasted until 1815—it was home to father-and-son Delaware River and Bay pilots Gilbert and Henry McCracken, who both served in a militia protecting Lewes from the British.

Beginning in March 1813, the British blockaded the Delaware coast. This would last for two years and have a major impact on trade and commerce. The Royal Navy's ships bombarded the town for two days that April, damaging many buildings. The Cannonball House is the lone survivor.

THE CANNONBALL HOUSE

WHAT: The historic Cannonball House of Lewes

WHERE: 118 Front St., Lewes, DE

COST: $5 per adult covers admission into all the Lewes Historical Society's museums. Children 12 and under are free.

PRO TIP: Hours may change; visit historiclewes.org for updated details.

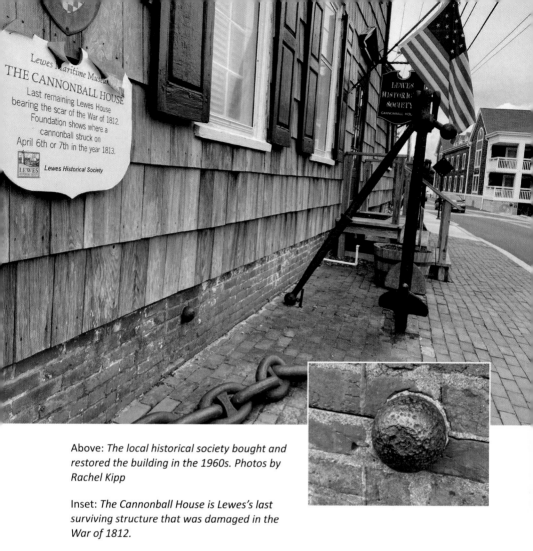

Lewes Maritime Museum

THE CANNONBALL HOUSE

Last remaining Lewes House bearing the scar of the War of 1812. Foundation shows where a cannonball struck on April 6th or 7th in the year 1813.

LEWES Lewes Historical Society

Above: *The local historical society bought and restored the building in the 1960s. Photos by Rachel Kipp*

Inset: *The Cannonball House is Lewes's last surviving structure that was damaged in the War of 1812.*

The Lewes Historical Society bought the home in 1963, during a period when many historic buildings in Lewes were being lost. The property then underwent significant restoration and preservation. "Old hand-hewn timbers are being used to make the restoration authentic," a newspaper writer from that time reported.

In its current incarnation as a museum, the Cannonball House is home to nautical art and maritime memorabilia, including a former lighthouse lens.

MOTHER CHURCH

What Delawarean played a critical role in founding America's independent Black churches?

Born a slave in Maryland in 1782, Peter Spencer gained his own freedom and then later founded the independence movement for Black churches.

Spencer moved to Wilmington in the 1790s and was educated in a school for "Free Africans." He joined and later became a community leader and lay preacher at Asbury Methodist Episcopal Church, which was predominantly White. At the time, it was illegal for Black people to worship without supervision from a White congregation.

Initially, Spencer and about 40 congregants left Asbury to start Ezion Methodist Episcopal Church, which was separate but still affiliated with the Methodist Episcopal denomination. But it eventually became clear that the denominational leadership would not allow the church to select its own leadership. In 1813, led by Spencer, the congregation decided to strike out on its own.

With the help of local abolitionists, including Underground Railroad conductor Thomas Garrett and the Quakers, Spencer's congregation was able to buy land on 9th and

BIRTHPLACE OF THE MOTHER CHURCH

WHAT: Site of the first Mother African Union First Colored Methodist Protestant Church and burial site of church founder Peter Spencer and his wife, Annes

WHERE: Peter Spencer Plaza, French Street between 8th and 9th Sts., Wilmington, DE

COST: Free

PRO TIP: August Quarterly is traditionally held the last week of each August and culminates with a Sunday worship service and "Big Quarterly," a concert in Wilmington's Tubman-Garrett Park featuring regional and nationally known gospel groups.

Left: *The site of Peter Spencer's first church in downtown Wilmington is now Peter Spencer Plaza, home to the sculpture "Father and Son." Photos by Rachel Kipp*

Right: *A sign at Spencer Plaza marks the gravesite of Peter Spencer and his wife, Annes.*

French Streets. The Union Church of African Members was the first independent Black church and denomination in the United States.

Spencer went on to found 30 other churches that became associated with the denomination, which later merged with an African Methodist Episcopal offshoot in Maryland in the 1860s. The denomination is now called the African Union First Colored Methodist Protestant Church or the "Spencer Churches."

Inspired by the "Big Meetings" of the Quakers, in 1814 Spencer founded the nation's longest-running Black heritage festival, August Quarterly. The festival became an outlet for worship as well as a social gathering and a time for Black people to discuss possible routes of escape from slavery. Today, August Quarterly is a week-long event that includes a ceremonial wreath-laying at Peter Spencer Plaza in Wilmington. That's the site of Spencer's first church, which was razed in the 1970s.

Though the original building is gone, Peter Spencer's Mother Africa Union Church is still in operation at 812 North Franklin Street in Wilmington, as is Ezion-Mount Carmel United Methodist Church, at 800 North Walnut Street.

THE PIRATES OF PYLE

How did a magazine illustrator singlehandedly create the modern image of the buccaneer?

Ask anyone how pirates are supposed to look, and even a small child can conjure up an image of men wearing headscarves, earrings, sashes, and shoes with sizable buckles.

While real-life pirates of the 18th century likely wore the same clothes as any sailor from that era, their distinctive look in pop culture sprang from the imagination of famed illustrator and Wilmington native Howard Pyle. Pyle's illustrations of historical scenes, American heroes, and fantastical figures appeared in books and popular magazines of the time, including *Harper's Weekly, Collier's*, and the *Saturday Evening Post*.

Part of what made his illustrations so popular was that Pyle infused every scene with a sense of realism—both through his research of the actual historical events he was depicting, and also by trying to think about the characters' emotions. To give his pirate illustrations a little drama and flash, Pyle combined period-accurate sailor clothing, such as blue coats and tri-cornered hats, with the traditional style of Spanish nomadic peoples.

The pirate illustrations clicked with readers, and in 1921 Pyle published his *Book of Pirates*, a compilation of his famous illustrations and stories of pirates' adventures. Decades later, production designers and costumers for Disney's *Pirates of*

Howard Pyle created such an epicenter for illustrators that his Franklin Street studio space wasn't large enough, so his protégés built the Schoonover Studios on nearby Rodney Street. Today the space is used for art appraisals, and also has a small gallery that is open to the public.

PYLE'S PIRATE LEGACY

High seas adventures were popular in the early 1900s, and many American artists were hired to illustrate pirate tales. Here, Frank Schoonover and Gayle Hoskins take on the subject. Notice how both artists use striking poses and splashes of red to tell their tales—lessons learned from their teacher, Howard Pyle.

One of Pyle's last major paintings, Marooned, 1909, features a lone pirate abandoned on a sandy beach. Marooned is one of the Delaware Art Museum's treasures, and it is currently on loan to the traveling exhibition, In American Waters: The Sea in American Painting. While Marooned is on the road, we are featuring pirate pictures by Pyle's students.

Howard Pyle (1853–1911)
Marooned, 1909
Oil on canvas
Museum Purchase, 1912
DAM 1912-136

Several of Howard Pyle's pirate paintings hang in the Delaware Art Museum in Wilmington. Photo by Rachel Kipp

PYLE'S PIRATES

WHAT: The former studios of illustrator Howard Pyle and his students, which are used by a painting group and as a resource for artists.

WHERE: 1305 N. Franklin St., Wilmington, DE

COST: Free

PRO TIP: The studios are open to the public during exhibits and by appointment.

the Caribbean movies studied Pyle's drawings for inspiration for the characters' clothing and environment.

In addition to creating an iconic style for pirates, Pyle was the first to draw Robin Hood wearing his now-trademark green hat and stockings, and is also responsible for what we now think of as "the look" of the Pilgrims and Revolutionary War soldiers.

The Wilmington Society of Fine Arts, the precursor to the Delaware Art Museum, was founded shortly after Pyle's death in 1911 to preserve and exhibit his work. Today, the museum's collection includes some of Pyle's pirate illustrations, along with a re-creation of the inside of his Wilmington studio. The museum also has works by some of Pyle's students, including N. C. Wyeth, Frank Schoonover, and Jessie Willcox Smith.

THE LAST SHIPS

What remains of Delaware's shipbuilding industry?

During the span of a century from the 1800s to the 1900s, Delaware was a major shipbuilding center, both coastal and inland. Four communities—Wilmington, Milford, Milton, and Bethel—played important roles in building and launching ships of all shapes and sizes.

Delaware's largest city, Wilmington, was home to four shipbuilders during the industry's height, from 1836 to the early 1900s. All were located along the Christiana River, with access to the critical ingredients of river and railroad. This turned into a major powerhouse for the war effort during World War II, with shipbuilder Dravo employing about 10,500 workers.

Milford, in south-central Delaware, had an earlier start, around 1782 along the Mispillion River. Nearby white oak stands were tapped for much-desired timbers, and the town once had seven shipyards operating at the same time. But steel and the railroads led to the industry shrinking, with the last major builder being the Vinyards. The company built patrol boats and other ships during both world wars. It stopped shipbuilding in 1951, but continued doing repairs into the early 1970s.

In Milton, along the Broadkill River to the south, shipbuilding began with smaller ships, such as sloops. The industry grew, fueled by its ready access to timber, and by the 1800s it was producing ocean-faring ships. By the 1890s, however, the industry was faltering with the rise of steam-powered vessels and timber shortages.

The site of Milford's Vinyard Shipyard is the focus of historic restoration and recreation efforts underway along the Mispillion River.

Above: *A public art project honoring Milford's maritime past led to the creation of colorful ships around the downtown area. Photo by Rachel Kipp*

Inset: *Abbott's shipyard on the Mispillion River in Milford, circa 1869. Photo courtesy of the Delaware Public Archives*

On the western side of the state, along Broad Creek, tiny Bethel became a major and improbable shipbuilding force. The town was known for its "sailing rams," three-masted shallow-draft schooners created to carry freight along the coast. It took workers a series of 10-hour days to build a ram in three months, primarily using hand tools. A single Bethel-built ship remains, the 1900-built *Victory Chimes*, originally the *Edwin and Maud*, which sails in Maine. "The town of Bethel probably owes its survival as a town to the wooden ships that were built here," historian Henry H. Hutchinson wrote in 1969.

SALUTE TO SHIPBUILDING

WHAT: The Mispillion Riverwalk in downtown Milford features public art of ship models decorated by local artists.

WHERE: South Walnut Street, Milford, DE

COST: n/a

PRO TIP: The Riverwalk is also home to Delaware's longest-running community farmers market, open from May to December on Saturday mornings.

HOT AND COLD CONFECTIONS

Why does this ice-cream shop make you sign a waiver before ordering?

This ice cream isn't for the faint of heart.

The Ice Cream Store, located just off the boardwalk in Rehoboth Beach, is known for its rotating menu of quirky ice-cream flavors. Owner Chip Hearn, who also has a business selling hot sauce, combined both of his passions when he started selling ice cream blended with fiery peppers.

In 2011, the store began featuring "Scorpion Sting," African vanilla ice cream flavored with cayenne pepper, cinnamon, "You Can't Handle This" hot sauce, and a strawberry sauce ribbon (with optional edible scorpion). The flavor was recognized by *Food Network Magazine* as its favorite scoop in Delaware.

Hearn topped himself a few years later when the store introduced Ghost Pepper Ice Cream—it used Scorpion Sting as its base and was so hot that customers were asked to sign a waiver before ordering. It was one of the most popular flavors at the shop.

More recently, the Ice Cream Store has featured Hot Scream Carolina Reaper Pepper, creamy vanilla ice cream colored bright red and topped with cinnamon, Ed's Carolina Reaper Pepper Mash, and a strawberry swirl.

In homage to part-time Rehoboth resident and noted ice-cream lover President Joe Biden, the Ice Cream Store menu features Biden's Summer White House Cherry, homemade vanilla ice cream with maraschino cherry juice and maraschino cherries.

Left: *During the summer, you can find long lines outside of the Ice Cream Store, but the expert staff whittles them down quickly. Photos by Rachel Kipp*

Right: *A partial list of the many flavors available at the shop, which sources its ice cream from the local institution Woodside Farm Creamery, in northern Delaware.*

And don't worry: less adventurous eaters can also find plenty of cool treats at the Ice Cream Store as well. There's your standard strawberry and vanilla, but there are also crazier flavors like "Crack" ("Brown Shugah" vanilla ice cream with pasteurized egg yolks, butter, and sea salt) and "Booger" (green Cake Batter ice cream with a green caramel swirl and marshmallow bits).

TREATS THAT BRING THE HEAT

WHAT: Ice cream laced with spicy peppers at the Ice Cream Store

WHERE: 6 Rehoboth Ave., Rehoboth Beach, DE

COST: Varies

PRO TIP: The store rotates flavors throughout the summer, and introduces new flavors every year—even if they don't have the exact one you're craving, there's plenty of delicious options to choose from!

BEACH BUG

What tiny insect is only found along Delaware's Atlantic coast?

The next time you visit Delaware's Atlantic coast and step outside after dusk, the flick-flick double flash of a firefly you see might not be visible anywhere else on the planet.

Delaware, and only Delaware, is home to the Bethany Beach firefly, a tiny creature that makes its home in freshwater habitat that's only found in a few places in the state, thanks to encroaching development.

The firefly's formal name is *Photuris bethaniensis*. It's under review for placement on the endangered-species list due to the pressures on its dwindling population.

There's a bit of a horror-movie backstory to the Bethany Beach firefly: females will flash their lights to attract males from other firefly species—and then chomp them up to pass the other species' defensive toxins to their babies.

The firefly lives in six places along the coast known as "interdunal swales," which are low-lying areas between sand dunes, so your chances of seeing them are slim. Those places are located in Delaware state parks.

The species' presence had not been recorded since it was first noted in 1953, but was rediscovered in the late 1990s by

THE BETHANY BEACH FIREFLY

WHAT: Delaware's unique firefly population

WHERE: It's found in three state parks: Cape Henlopen, Delaware Seashore, and Fenwick Island.

COST: Park entrance fees are in effect from March 1 to November 30 each year; see destateparks.com for current rates.

PRO TIP: Don't walk on sand dunes to find the fireflies—that damages the coast's protective barriers.

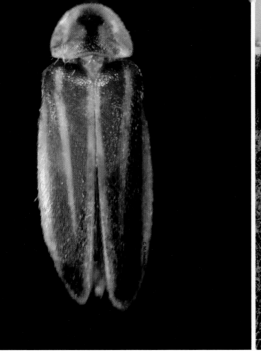

Left: *The Bethany Beach firefly had not been spotted for about four decades when Delaware State University scientist Christopher Heckscher rediscovered it. Photos by Christopher Heckscher*

Right: *The firefly is found in just six places in the state, all "interdunal swales" such as this area.*

a scientist at Delaware State University, Christopher Heckscher. He recalled the experience to a journalist two decades later: "I figured if there's a rare firefly, it's probably associated with a rare wetland. I'm pretty sure we found it on our first night out."

The Bethany Beach firefly is one of approximately 170 firefly species found in North America.

DELAWARE ON GUARD

How did the First State defend the coast against Nazis during World War II?

One of the first things you spot from many points along Delaware's Atlantic coast are the towers, concrete structures up to 90 feet tall with viewing slits from which to see for miles.

Built to guard Delaware's coast and Delaware River shipping from the Nazis, the fire towers were not intended to fire on the enemy themselves, but to locate and target ships using the artillery based at Fort Miles, a sprawling complex occupying what is now Cape Henlopen State Park.

There, concealed in towering sand dunes, were mighty bunkers and gun emplacements ready to defend the homeland against Hitler's potential invasion or U-boats going after shipping routes.

Fort Miles spanned 1,000 acres of the cape, with more than 2,000 staff assigned there. It had barracks, a gym, and a hospital, in addition to the multiple gun batteries and fire towers. There were 11 towers in Delaware and four across the bay in Cape May, New Jersey. Underwater, there were giant magnetic coils that gave an early warning signal, as well as sea mines at the Delaware Bay entrance.

DELAWARE ON GUARD

WHAT: Fort Miles Museum and Historical Area at Cape Henlopen State Park

WHERE: 15099 Cape Henlopen Dr., Lewes, DE

COST: Park entrance fees are in effect from March 1 to November 30 each year; see destateparks.com for current rates.

PRO TIP: The museum is located inside Battery 519, open during scheduled tours and open-house events. Visit destateparks.com/FortMiles for up-to-date information and schedules.

Left: *One of the buildings used to house troops and activities at Fort Miles, now part of the Fort Miles Historical Area. Photo by Dan Shortridge*

Right Top: *Battery Hunter was a gun battery at Fort Miles and later home to an anti-sub listening system. It now sits underneath a platform for hawk-spotting. Photo by Dan Shortridge*

Right Bottom: *Winterized tents kept soldiers at Fort Miles warm against the chill winter winds coming off the Atlantic and the Delaware Bay. Photo courtesy of the Delaware Public Archives*

Ultimately, the invasion never came, so the guns were never fired at an enemy. The fort did see some Germans when a surrendering U-boat crew was kept there temporarily. A US prize crew brought the U-boat right up to what is now the fishing pier at the state park. Today, history enthusiasts sometimes reenact the crew's surrender at special events.

During the Cold War, Fort Miles was home to a missile-watching radar site, antennae to improve long-range communication after a nuclear attack, and a listening station to track Soviet submarines.

THE WATCHTOWERS

Where did firespotters keep watch from on high?

In the 1920s, Delaware was covered in forests—about a third of the land was wooded.

But from 1928 to 1931, a series of horrific fires reduced the 423,000 acres of woodlands by about 10,000. Pine trees and cypress trees were turned to ash by the blazes. (Pun not intended.)

To keep that from occurring again, Delaware and Maryland jointly erected a series of seasonally manned watchtowers to protect the land from high above.

The firespotters were up in their seats only temporarily, from March to May and again from October to December. They were given phones, radios, maps, and a device called an alidade that let them pinpoint the location of a smoke plume.

In Sussex County, home to most of the blazes, officials built towers at Dagsboro, Laurel, Ellendale, and Woodenhawk, the last an unincorporated place on the state line with Maryland along Route 404. Eventually there were six towers in operation.

The Woodenhawk tower was jointly operated by Maryland and Delaware, and is the only one still standing, though closed and inaccessible to the public. Delaware's towers were all closed in the mid-1970s, and all but Woodenhawk were eventually dismantled and removed for safety reasons. Maryland stopped using its towers in 1983, with many still standing.

Today Delaware is home to about 370,000 acres of forests. The state government has a robust open space protection program.

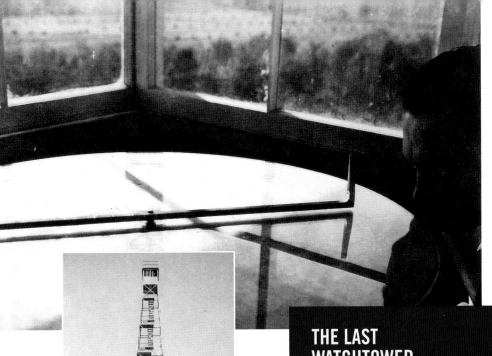

Top: *This device, called an alidade, helped watchers locate a telltale plume of smoke from their high perches. Photos courtesy of the Delaware Forest Service*

Inset: *The Woodenhawk firetower, shown in 1931, is the last one remaining in Delaware.*

"We're in a very flat area. And we're so populated, someone's going to see," said Delaware State Forester Michael Valenti.

THE LAST WATCHTOWER

WHAT: The Woodenhawk watchtower

WHERE: US Rt. 404, at the Delaware-Maryland state line. If you're driving into Maryland, it's a short way past Little Wagon Produce.

COST: n/a

PRO TIP: Today, the Delaware Forest Service operates a wildland fire crew that travels to other states to help with forest fires. Volunteer recruits are always needed; visit agriculture.delaware.gov/forest-service/wildland-crew/ to sign up.

SECRET WARRIORS

What WWII weapons were quietly developed at a nondescript hangar in Dover?

Today, the idea of rockets being launched from aircraft seems simple. But during World War II, the concept was revolutionary.

The US Army Air Forces, as our main military service for aerial combat and activities was then known, formed a special unit following research in Maryland and Ohio. It was located at Dover Army Air Field, now Dover Air Force Base, and activated in April 1944.

The military research team had a broad mandate: to develop, create, and test any ways to fire rockets from aircraft, including from bombers. The unit had a combined hangar, shop area, and power-plant operation known as Building 1301. It also had a barracks, mess hall, ammunition area, and firing range. Later in 1944, an experimental range for rockets was created in California, under the command of the Dover team.

HANGAR 1301

WHAT: Former home to a secret World War II rocket program

WHERE: Now the Air Mobility Command Museum, it's at 1301 Heritage Rd., Dover AFB, Dover, DE

COST: Free

PRO TIP: Don't try to enter through the main Dover Air Force Base gate! The airmen won't appreciate that.

The Dover rocket range used for test firing was on the land now occupied by the Bombay Hook National Wildlife Refuge.

Top: *Hangar 1301 is now home to the indoor exhibits at the Air Mobility Command Museum on the grounds of Dover Air Force Base. Photo by Dan Shortridge*

Inset: *P-47 Thunderbolts in the hangar at Dover's "Rocket Center" were equipped with the new rockets. Photo courtesy of the Delaware Public Archives*

The unit was eventually tasked with arming a squad of Thunderbolts—P-47 fighter-bombers—to be used against tanks and guns that bombers couldn't get at.

After the end of the war, 1301 was used as a regular fighter hangar until the 1970s. It was then used as a storage building and suffered from neglect, but was restored in the early 1990s. Hangar 1301 became part of the National Register of Historic Places in 1994 and home to the Air Mobility Command Museum in 1996.

BLACK BRAVERY

How did a courageous family take on neighborhood racists?

159 days.

That's how long the Rayfield family lived in their home outside the town of New Castle, having moved there to live closer to their father's job and to expand his side garbage-collection business.

On the 160th day, the home was bombed.

With their house destroyed and no longer fit for human habitation, the Rayfield family left the neighborhood of Collins Park after that day in 1959.

The vicious attack is a reminder of how integration in Delaware did not go smoothly, and how little time has passed since overt White supremacy dominated politics, power, and the headlines.

The August 2 bombing was the fourth violent attempt by racists to chase the Rayfields out. Bullets were shot through a window, a fire was set, and an earlier bombing attempt failed after labor union members helped them rebuild.

The Rayfields were greeted on their move-in day by an angry mob of 300 segregationists who opposed a Black family's right to exist in the all-White enclave. It didn't shake them.

"We bought it and we intend to stay here," Lucille Rayfield defiantly informed a reporter the next day.

She, her husband, George, and daughter, Geraldine, stood up to the hatred for just over five months. Even after

BLACK BRAVERY

WHAT: Historic marker near the site of the 1959 Collins Park bombing

WHERE: 1 Killoran Dr., New Castle, DE

COST: n/a

PRO TIP: The Rayfields' former home was located at 107 Bellanca Lane.

Left: *Today, 107 Bellanca Lane, where the Rayfields' home stood, is an empty garden lot.*
Photos by Dan Shortridge

Right: *A historic marker stands outside of the Collins Park neighborhood commemorating the Rayfields' courage.*

their house was reduced to fragments—the three Rayfields had thankfully been out visiting family—they still projected resistance.

"I don't want to comment," Lucille said while looking over the rubble of their former home. "I don't want those . . . to think they got me."

Ed Palm was a young boy living in the neighborhood then. Five decades later, he recalled with regret that his mother was a segregationist and leader in the fight against the Rayfields.

"Her 15 minutes of fame came when she was shown on local television shaking a finger in a reporter's face and opining that 'the colored turn everywhere they live into a slum,'" Palm, who is White, wrote in a newspaper column.

Several men were later arrested and convicted on charges related to both bombings.

The lot still stands empty, a mute testament to one family's courage and the hatred they had to endure.

The state erected a historic marker near the site in 2017, the first time that such a relatively recent event had been so memorialized.

REVOLUTIONARY WRITER

Who was the Delawarean known as the "Penman of the Revolution"?

Few people were as hated during the American Revolutionary era as John Dickinson. He couldn't seem to get a break, walking a thin line between the battles.

To the Loyalists, he was a traitor to the Crown; to some Patriots, he was sympathetic to the British. His plantation in Delaware was ransacked and his Philadelphia home burned.

Over the decades, he earned the nickname "the Penman of the Revolution" for his extensive writings.

But historian Jane Calvert, who has made a study of Dickinson's life and works, says he was not a rabidly pro-independence activist. "He did not want revolution," she said. "He was writing to prevent a revolution," working toward a goal of reconciling with England.

Dickinson, born on the Eastern Shore of Maryland in 1732, served in every national assembly starting with the Stamp Act Congress and going to the Constitutional Convention. He opposed many taxation acts from across the pond. He served in the Delaware Assembly as its speaker and also in the Pennsylvania Assembly. Dickinson enlisted in the militia as a private, but declined to sign the Declaration of Independence.

After independence, John Dickinson served as a leader in two states. In 1781, he was elected president of Delaware—equivalent to governor today—and then, while still serving, he was named president of Pennsylvania.

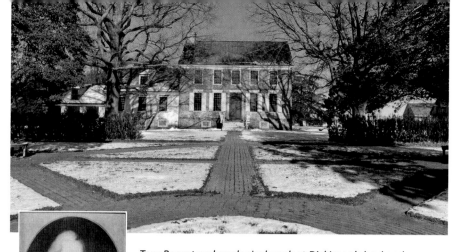

Top: *Recent archaeological work at Dickinson's boyhood home, outside Dover, found a burial site believed to be that of enslaved people. Photo by Dan Shortridge*

Inset: *John Dickinson was a farmer and prolific writer. Photo courtesy of the National Archives*

His "Letters from a Farmer in Pennsylvania," published in 1767–68, were a clarion call to the colonists: "A dreadful stroke is aimed at the liberty of these colonies," he wrote. "For the cause of one is the cause of all."

Dickinson died in 1808 and is buried in Wilmington. Today he is remembered in Delaware at the Dickinson Plantation, his childhood home, where his father is laid to rest and which is a state historical site.

In 2021, state officials announced the discovery of a Black burial site on the plantation grounds, likely the graves of the people enslaved by the Dickinson family. Though John Dickinson himself legally granted freedom to the people he enslaved by 1786, the ongoing research and work is another reminder of the gaps between the words of liberty and freedom and the way in which the founding generations lived.

PENMAN'S HOME

WHAT: The John Dickinson Plantation, childhood home of John Dickinson

WHERE: 340 Kitts Hummock Rd., Dover, DE

COST: Free

PRO TIP: Check history. delaware.gov for updated hours and days of operation. Reservations may be needed.

IMPRISONED ON THE ISLAND

Who spent the Civil War as prisoners on an island in the middle of the bay?

Thousands of captured Confederate soldiers spent part of the Civil War imprisoned in Fort Delaware, located on Pea Patch Island in the middle of the Delaware Bay. The site was chosen because Fort Delaware, built in the mid-1800s to protect the First State and nearby Philadelphia from attack, was state-of-the-art for the times and also relatively isolated.

Many of those captured at the battle at Gettysburg were imprisoned on Pea Patch Island.

At one point in the war, as many as 16,000 Confederates were held at Fort Delaware, suffering in desperate and decrepit conditions. Fort Delaware was run by Gen. Albin F. Schoepf, who was called "General Terror" by the soldiers for depriving prisoners of food and water and allowing disease to run rampant.

Legend has it that many of the men who died at Fort Delaware, and even some who survived, still haunt Pea Patch Island. Ghost hunters—including those from the A&E television show of the same name—have been doing investigations and leading public tours there for years.

THE MOST HAUNTED SPOT IN DELAWARE

WHAT: Fort Delaware, a former Civil War prison camp on Pea Patch Island in the Delaware Bay

WHERE: Pea Patch Island is only reachable by ferry; the dock is located at 45 Clinton St. in Delaware City, DE

COST: Varies

PRO TIP: Book your spot on one of the ghost hunting tours early—they sell out quickly!

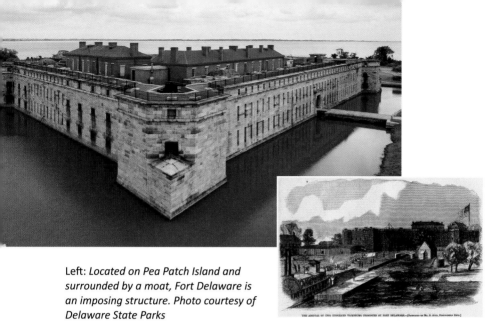

Left: *Located on Pea Patch Island and surrounded by a moat, Fort Delaware is an imposing structure. Photo courtesy of Delaware State Parks*

Right: *An 1863 illustration from Harper's Weekly captured Fort Delaware during its years as a Civil War prison. Photo courtesy of the Delaware Public Archives*

A park employee told the local newspaper in 2006 that staff had seen a woman in work clothes walk through a wall from kitchen to pantry. During the Ghost Hunters episode filmed on Pea Patch Island, the team heard cannon fire inside some of the fort's tunnels, saw a ghostly man peeking around a corner with the use of a thermal imaging camera, and heard the sounds of rattling chains throughout their investigation.

Each fall, Fort Delaware offers paranormal tours so members of the public can try their luck at ghost hunting. During Fort Delaware's spring-to-fall season, you can also visit during the day and take tours focused on the less-spooky history of the spot.

In addition to possible ghosts, Pea Patch Island is also home to one of the largest bird-nesting areas on the East Coast, including nine different species of herons, egrets, and ibis.

MILES'S STOMPIN' GROUNDS

How did this entertainment venue end up with a monster as its mascot?

The one-mile concrete, banked oval track at Dover International Speedway earned the nickname "The Monster Mile" soon after it opened in 1969, due to how demanding it was on drivers and their equipment.

A few decades later, from the nickname came the venue's mascot, a red-eyed monster named Miles. Visit the speedway and you'll see Miles everywhere, including on memorabilia, race tickets, and the sizable cement monster trophy given to the winner of the NASCAR Cup Series race held in Dover at least once a year.

The most prominent manifestation of Miles is at Victory Plaza, where a 46-foot tall fiberglass monster appears to burst out of a circular base behind the grandstand of the front stretch of the track. This version of Miles (which has red eyes that light up at night and can be seen from Delaware Route 1, about a half-mile away) was unveiled in 2008 as part of the speedway's $6 million "Monster Makeover." The monster's base includes

---

When the Miles statue was first built, it held a red-and-white stock car in its hand. In 2016, a blue Number 43 Smithfield Foods car was swapped in after the company signed a sponsor agreement. In 2020, financial-services company Ally became the statue sponsor and an Ally Number 48 Chevy Camaro was placed in Miles's hand.

In Miles's massive hand is a full-sized stock car. Photo courtesy of Nigel Kinrade Photography

plaques that honor notable Dover International Speedway drivers. In one hand, Miles holds aloft a full-size stock car.

Miles even ran for the White House, albeit with an unsuccessful campaign, in 2012 using the slogan "Concrete for Change." The track's historian acted as his campaign manager.

MILES THE MONSTER

WHAT: A 46-foot tall fiberglass statue of Miles the Monster, mascot of Dover International Speedway

WHERE: 1131 N. Dupont Hwy., Dover, DE. The monster can be reached by making a left at the Speedway main entrance, then going to the right, and driving around the stadium to the back side.

COST: Free

PRO TIP: Miles's big day comes every May, when a NASCAR Cup Series race is held in Dover.

SEPARATE SCHOOLS

What's the story behind Delaware's former system of segregated schools?

During the days of segregation, when Black and White students were forced into separate schools by law, Delaware featured a school system unique to the state—funded by a millionaire.

From the 1910s and '20s until after *Brown v. Board of Education* in 1954, Black children in Delaware were taught by Black teachers across the state in 92 school buildings known as "colored schools," also dubbed "du Pont schools" after their founder and funder, Pierre S. du Pont.

The schools were small and located in rural areas, but featured indoor toilets, heat, and windows. They cost the millionaire du Pont about $30 million in today's dollars.

After desegregation, the schools were closed as the White schools became integrated. White-controlled school districts chose what to do with the buildings, which meant no one documented their histories and heritage at that time.

A century after the first schools were built, many had been torn down or moved. Some had been converted into private homes, some taken over by school districts, and some simply stood vacant.

One such school was the Ross Point School, outside of Laurel. Known as School 215-C, it never had fewer than 20 students, and one year, the late legendary teacher Cora Selby taught 43 students, all in one class. Selby, who taught there from 1941 until its closure, once recalled how the students

One school that has been preserved is the Iron Hill School, near Newark, which closed in 1965 and is now owned by a science and history museum.

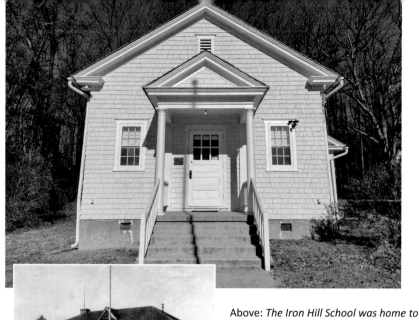

Above: *The Iron Hill School was home to a local science and history museum until recently. Photo by Dan Shortridge*

Inset: *The Ross Point School, seen in 1922, closed in 1964 and was heavily damaged by a fire in 2007. Photo courtesy of the Delaware Public Archives*

and their families formed a community: "They had all the respect in the world for the teacher and the preacher."

Selby and Ross Point's trustees objected to consolidation with Laurel's White schools after 1954. Their students got new textbooks each year, and they knew the anger they would face from White racism once Black students were integrated. But in 1964, Ross Point closed. Despite efforts to restore it, the building remained empty and burned in 2007.

SEPARATE SCHOOLS

WHAT: School 112-C, owned by the Iron Hill Science Center

WHERE: 1115 Robert L. Melson Lane, Newark, DE

COST: Admission is $2, with kids under 6 and seniors free

PRO TIP: For a full history of the schools featuring the perspectives of former students and teachers, view the documentary *A Separate Place*, produced by graduate Dr. Jeanne Nutter: www.hagley.org/research/separate-place.

MUSKRAT ON THE MENU

How did muskrat become a (questionable) Delaware delicacy?

Forget scrapple, Grotto Pizza, or Capriotti's Bobbie sandwich—the true quintessential Delaware delicacy just might be the muskrat dinner.

Muskrats, or marsh rabbits, are cuddly-looking, marsh-dwelling rodents; they grow to be about 25 inches long and eat marsh grass, keeping it from clogging waterways. In the wintertime, snow and ice flatten marsh grasses and make it easier to spot muskrat lodges, which is how the rodents initially became a wintertime staple on the Delmarva Peninsula. Early settlers learned about the muskrat from Native American tribes, and in the first part of the 20th century, hunting muskrats for their pelts was big business in the area.

Seasonal muskrat dinners used to be a tradition across Delmarva, but now they've dwindled to just a few local restaurants and community centers. That may be in part because muskrat is an acquired taste. One area dining critic described it as a "dark, earthy meat" with a "brackish, fishy flavor that lingers like a houseguest who has long overstayed his welcome."

One local restaurant that still offers this taste of local history is the Southern Grille in Ellendale, Sussex County. It's on the

---

Smyrna's since-closed Wagon Wheel restaurant famously refused to remove its muskrat dinner from the menu when Food Network star Robert Irvine renovated the eatery on the series *Restaurant: Impossible.*

Left: *Muskrat lodges can be more easily spotted during the wintertime. Photo courtesy of the US Fish & Wildlife Service*

Right: *Cooked "head on" muskrat doesn't exactly look appetizing, but devoted Delaware connoisseurs swear by it. Photo by Dan Shortridge*

menu every winter during muskrat hunting season. You can get it head on or head off, boiled, fried, or barbecued, and served with or without gravy. And don't worry; your less-adventurous dining companions will also have plenty to choose from on the menu, including fried chicken, chicken and dumplings, and prime rib.

DELAWARE DELICACY

WHAT: Muskrat dinners at the Southern Grille

WHERE: 711 Main St., Ellendale, DE

COST: The muskrat dinner costs $17.95

PRO TIP: Muskrat season runs from late November through March.

CLUCK, CLUCK, OOPS

What mistake led to the birth of a multimillion-dollar agricultural sector?

In the early 1900s, chickens were mostly raised for the eggs they produced. They were cooked and eaten when they couldn't lay any longer, but the meat was tough, not tender like today.

In the small community of Ocean View, Cecile and Wilmer Steele kept a flock of hens for laying, like many fellow small-scale farmers. But an error one day in 1923 would lead to the creation of an entirely new industry.

As the story goes, Cecile Steele ordered 50 new chicks to replenish her flocks. She received 500.

What to do with 450 extra chicks? Might as well raise them and try to sell the meat. In the meantime, she put the chicks in a piano box while a shed was built.

A few months later, the Steeles were selling the meat at 62 cents per pound. In today's dollars, that was about $8,300 from the misdelivered flock. Three years later, the Steeles were growing 10,000 birds, and their neighbors were catching on to this new business opportunity. Farmers quickly dropped egg laying and began raising so-called "broiler" chickens year-round.

There were several factors that helped support the growth of the meat-chicken industry in Delaware, including low labor and building costs, a mild climate, and the area's proximity to

---

The Steeles didn't just rely on chickens for their income; Wilmer Steele had a job with the US Coast Guard. But within a few years after their first venture, he quit and began working full-time growing chickens and building broiler houses.

A chicken house owned by Cecile Steele shows just how small-scale the poultry industry was in the early days. Photo by Dan Shortridge

larger markets where the birds could be sold, according to the late historian Bill Williams.

Today, more than 1,200 farmers on the Delmarva Peninsula raise more than 570 million chickens each year, contracting with processing companies such as Perdue, Mountaire, and Allen Harim. What began as an accidental zero on a shipment has created tens of thousands of jobs across the region.

Tragically, the Steeles died in 1940 when their yacht— purchased with the proceeds from their chicken empire—exploded off the coast of Maryland.

CECILE STEELE'S CHICKEN HOUSE

WHAT: A broiler chicken house once used by the Steeles

WHERE: The Delaware Agricultural Museum & Village, 850 North DuPont Hwy., Dover, DE

COST: $5 ages 18 and up, $3 ages 6-17, free ages 5 and under

PRO TIP: The museum also features an outdoor 1890s village to visit and explore.

DELAWARE VS. DELAWARE

How did two First State politicos end up running for the presidency at the same time?

In the late 1980s, as the Reagan Administration was winding down, the race for the White House was completely wide open—from both the Republican and Democratic sides—for the first time since 1968. With no incumbent running in the 1988 election, many politicians tossed their hats in the ring for a shot at the presidency—including two from Delaware.

On the Republican side, one of the hopefuls was former Delaware Governor and Congressman Pierre S. "Pete" du Pont IV, who launched his 1988 campaign before anyone else, in 1986. Possessed of a famous name and family wealth, du Pont's platform included school vouchers, drug testing for high schoolers, and a private option to Social Security. He won the backing of New Hampshire's *Union Leader* newspaper, but didn't catch on with voters, coming in next-to-last in New Hampshire and Iowa. Du Pont passed away in May 2021 at age 86.

Delaware's Democratic contender was Joseph Robinette Biden Jr., then a US senator. Regarded as a strong orator and prolific fundraiser—he entered the race with more than $2 million on hand, more than any of his Democratic opponents—Biden ranked at 3–4 percent in the polls nationally when he announced his candidacy in June 1987. But his campaign was

---

Joe Biden tried again for the presidency in 2008, and was picked as Barack Obama's vice president. In 2020, the third time became the charm, as he won the prize he'd chased for more than three decades.

Top: *Vice President Joe Biden is sworn in for the start of the second Obama-Biden term in 2013. Photo courtesy of the White House David Lienemann*

Bottom: *Delaware Gov. Pete du Pont served as the state's chief executive from 1977 to 1985. Photo courtesy of the Delaware Public Archives*

hit with plagiarism scandals, including accusations that he had not attributed words to other politicians on the stump and in a law-school paper. Amid the furor, Biden dropped out in September 1987, before any votes had been cast.

One wonders what might have happened had both du Pont and Biden won their party's nominations and gone head-to-head. How would Delaware have voted?

LASTING LEGACIES

WHAT: Both men established organizations to carry on their work. The Pete du Pont Freedom Foundation works to promote private enterprise and innovation. Biden has two centers, the Penn Biden Center for Diplomacy and Global Engagement at the University of Pennsylvania and the Biden Institute at the University of Delaware (part of the Biden School of Public Policy & Administration).

WHERE: Pete du Pont Freedom Foundation: www. petedupontfreedomfoundation. org/pete-du-pont/

Penn Biden Center: global. upenn.edu/penn-biden-center

Biden Institute: www. bidenschool.udel.edu/ bideninstitute

COST: n/a

PRO TIP: The du Pont Foundation holds a regular competition for entrepreneurs, while the Biden Institute's core issues include civil liberties, health care access, and preventing violence against women.

DEATH BY CHOCOLATE

Where did the infamous "chocolate candy murders" take place?

The crime is largely forgotten now, but at the turn of the last century, it shocked the nation.

The "chocolate candy murders," as they were known, resulted in the death of two women—by way of poisoned chocolates, marking the first time the US mail had been used for that heinous of a crime.

The story begins with the marriage of Mary Elizabeth Pennington and John Dunning. She was the daughter of a former congressman and state attorney general; he was a newspaper reporter who tired of the dull life in Delaware and soon moved his wife and baby daughter to San Francisco.

Unfortunately for all, Dunning was a drinker, gambler, and womanizer, which all came to a head in California. He began an affair with a woman named Cordelia Botkin, and by 1896 had lost his job with the Associated Press after stealing to settle his gambling losses.

Faced with an unemployed cheater of a husband, Mary took their daughter and returned to Delaware. Dunning and Botkin were shacked up in a hotel, still in California, but the ne'er-do-well journalist apparently had a change of heart, telling his lover that he was leaving her to go back to his wife.

Then one August day, a package was delivered for Mary in Delaware, with a note inside: "With Love to Yourself and

Arrested at her home in San Francisco, Cordelia Botkin reportedly declared: "The chagrin is past. The horror is over. I have suffered all the humiliation. I am ready."

The Pennington home, where sisters Mary Dunning and Ida Deane ate poisoned chocolates and died, is now home to the state housing agency. Some employees think the building is haunted. Photo by Dan Shortridge

DEATH BY CHOCOLATE

WHAT: The site of the "chocolate candy murders"

WHERE: The former Pennington house, now the offices of the Delaware State Housing Authority, 18-20 The Green, Dover, DE

COST: n/a

PRO TIP: Mary Dunning and Ida Deane are buried in the Old Presbyterian Cemetery, 316 S. Governors Ave., Dover, about a five-minute walk away.

Baby," signed "Mrs. C." The box of chocolates was shared widely with friends and family relaxing on the porch.

In a matter of days, both Mary Dunning and her sister Ida Deane were dead.

Their father, the state's former top law enforcement official, had the delicacies tested. The lab found arsenic. Dunning, now a widower, was recalled from covering the Spanish-American War to inspect the note and earlier threatening letters, and immediately pegged Botkin as the culprit.

Botkin was tried in California twice and convicted both times, in 1898 and 1904. Sentenced to life behind bars, she died in 1910 in San Quentin. Dunning died two years prior.

"This was one of those trials of the century—much like the Scopes Trial or the O.J. Simpson case," recalled state historic interpreter Sarah Zimmerman.

BEAN POWER

Why does the state grow so many lima beans?

Delaware is a tiny state, and the lima is a tiny bean. They're meant for each other. So it makes sense that the state's farmers grow more lima beans destined for the freezer aisle or cans than any other state—a full third of the nation's total.

They are, says former state agriculture secretary and lima-bean researcher Ed Kee, "a cornerstone crop."

About 50 farmers plant limas on 15,000 acres, mainly in central and southern Delaware, with the beans headed to processing companies. From there, they end up in freezer bags across the country, and then in succotash and other dishes on dining-room tables.

Delaware's land is well-suited for the bean due to high humidity levels and moderate temperatures. Historically, the state had a thriving canning industry, today replaced with freezing operations.

BIG BEANS

WHAT: Lima bean fields

WHERE: Delaware lima beans are grown on fields in Kent and Sussex counties, primarily on the eastern side of both counties.

COST: Free

PRO TIP: Catch a glimpse of the harvest along Delaware's Rt. 1 from late August to October, with large harvesters moving slowly through the fields.

Lima beans originated in the tropical regions of Central and South America, and made their way here via Native American trading routes. They were on the continent long before the European colonists.

Hanover Foods is a large processor of lima beans with a facility in the state. Photo by Rachel Kipp

There are three types of limas grown in Delaware: green baby limas, larger Fordhook beans, and "pole beans," which are primarily eaten fresh.

Delaware is also a primary center for lima-bean research, which takes place at the University of Delaware's center outside Georgetown. Scientists there are testing different ways to protect against heat and pests.

A FAMILY FEUD?

Why do jagged shards of glass surround one of Delaware's most famous estates?

If the light is right, drivers along Delaware Route 141 may be distracted by a sparkling glint atop a tall wall of stone.

It's the wall surrounding the impressively grand Nemours estate, once owned by Alfred I. du Pont. The sparkles come from sharp shards of colored glass embedded into the top of the 10-foot-tall wall.

Local lore has it that the glass was installed by du Pont to keep out intruders—members of his own family with whom the wealthy industrialist was feuding.

Any story about the du Ponts must distinguish which du Ponts are being discussed. Alfred I. du Pont was a co-founder, with cousins Pierre S. and T. Coleman, of the Du Pont Co.

Alfred I. du Pont modeled the 77-room Nemours estate after a palace of Marie Antoinette on the grounds of Versailles. The cost of the 1909–10 project was $2 million, worth more than $52 million today.

The wall around its 300 acres went up between 1915 and 1916 for increased privacy and security. One biographer reported that children were paid for bottles—one cent each—which were then broken and the shards set up high.

Today, the Nemours estate is also home to Nemours Children's Hospital, which occupies 50 acres of the property.

Left: *The glass shards are only visible from the road if you're looking directly at them or the light catches them just so. Photos by Dan Shortridge*

Right: *The wall stretches all the way around the Nemours estate, now also home to a famed children's hospital.*

Inset: *The top of the wall has divots where shards of glass were placed.*

GLASS-TOPPED WALL

WHAT: The Nemours Estate

WHERE: 1600 Rockland Rd., Wilmington, DE

COST: Day and season passes are available; costs vary.

PRO TIP: The estate closes for part of the year during the winter and reopens in the spring. Check nemoursestate.org for details and dates.

But there's no concrete evidence to support either the family-feud idea or the child-bottle-bounty story, historians say today. It's pure speculation, though a story that's lasted for generations.

Alfred I. du Pont, who passed away in 1935, is buried with his wife, brother-in-law, and dog underneath the imposing 210-foot-tall bell tower on the estate's grounds.

ROAD TO THE WHITE HOUSE

How did this highway rest stop come to play tribute to two US presidents?

Most highway rest stops are good for a quick break to buy drinks or gas during a long day on the road, but Delaware's Biden Welcome Center has a unique—and presidential—history.

First, the obvious White House connection: in 2018, then-former Vice President Joe Biden, wife Jill, daughter Ashley and sister Valerie Biden Owens were on hand when the I-95 rest stop was renamed in the family's honor.

A PRESIDENTIAL REST STOP

WHAT: Biden Welcome Center rest stop

WHERE: 530 John F. Kennedy Memorial Hwy., Newark, DE 19702

COST: Free

PRO TIP: The rest stop is accessible from both the north and southbound lanes of I-95; going southbound you can exit at Delaware 896 to avoid paying a toll at the Maryland state line.

At the ceremony, Biden called it "one of the most meaningful things that has happened to our family." Cut to November 2020, when Biden was elected 46th president of the United States. The rest stop, with its prominently displayed "Biden" signs, became the site of numerous photo ops.

But the rest stop also has a connection to a second president, John F. Kennedy. In 1963, just days before Kennedy was assassinated, the White House helicopter landed on the nearby Delaware-Maryland border and Kennedy participated in the ribbon-cutting for the opening of two stretches of I-95, the 59-mile Maryland Northeastern Expressway and the 11-mile Delaware Turnpike.

Left: *A bust of President John F. Kennedy is displayed at the rest stop. Photos by Rachel Kipp*

Right: *After President Joe Biden's victory in 2020, travelers began snapping frequent photos outside of the building.*

After Kennedy's death, the two states decided to rename the two sections of highway in Kennedy's honor. The 1964 dedication ceremony took place in the "Hot Shoppes" restaurant inside the Delaware rest stop and a bust of JFK was unveiled in the rest-stop lobby.

The rest stop was completely rebuilt in 2010, but there's still a small display inside the Biden Welcome Center commemorating JFK's speech.

Among the other locales in the First State that pay tribute to the Bidens are the train station in Wilmington and the Biden Environmental Training Center at Cape Henlopen State Park.

ANCIENT BLOODLINES

What prehistoric sea creature is vital to modern medical advances?

In the early days of modern medicine, ensuring that drugs are safe was a daunting prospect. The process often involved experimentation on rabbits.

That was how it worked in 1956 when scientists developed an entirely new testing system—using the blood of a sea creature that's more ancient than dinosaurs. The lowly horseshoe crab, which has scared generations of kids along the Delaware seashore with its long spiky-looking tail, is the keystone to ensuring the safety of everyone who's gotten a vaccine.

Today, horseshoe crabs are captured and taken to a laboratory—there are five companies that handle the crabs—where up to a third of their bright-blue blood is drained. They're then returned to the sea. The blood is transformed into a testing solution that verifies vaccines are contamination-free.

It's not painless for the crabs, however; bled female horseshoe crabs are less likely to reproduce, while 10-30 percent of bled crabs die.

In the words of science journalist Alexis Madrigal, it's a "forgettable sea creature with a hidden chemical superpower."

HORSESHOE CRABS

WHAT: Seeing horseshoe crabs during spawning season

WHERE: At high tide along the Delaware Bay coastline, particularly Kitts Hummock, Bowers Beach and Slaughter Beach; prime season is from mid-May to mid-June

COST: Free

PRO TIP: If you see a horseshoe crab stranded on its back, just flip it— but not by its tail.

Top: *Before scientists tapped their blood, horseshoe crabs (or "king crabs") were harvested for fertilizer and feed, such as these near Bowers Beach in 1928. Photo courtesy of the Delaware Public Archives*

Inset: *Horseshoe crabs may look frightening, but they're perfectly harmless—and incredibly helpful to science. Photo by Rachel Kipp*

Long before horseshoe crab blood transformed pharmaceutical research, the crabs themselves were harvested by the millions around the Delaware Bay, used for fertilizer on farm fields and for hog feed. Today, they're used as bait for whelk.

Research is under way to create a synthetic replacement for horseshoe-crab blood. It's already on the market under the name PyroGene.

A ROUND FOR THE HISTORY BOOKS

Where can you see the spot where a group of delegates met to ratify the Constitution–and make Delaware the First State?

This quiet spot at the corner of State Street and the Green in downtown Dover was the site of some key moments in Delaware's—and the nation's—history.

The Golden Fleece Tavern was built in the 1730s. Run by Elizabeth Battell, the tavern's location in the middle of the state made it a convenient meeting spot and place to pass information. When Dover became the state capital in 1777, the Legislative Council, the Assembly's upper house, met there until the first state house was completed in 1791.

Perhaps the most notable day in Golden Fleece history was December 5, 1787, when a document detailing a framework for governing a new country, the United States, arrived from Philadelphia. Ten delegates from each of Delaware's three counties met at the tavern to review what would become the US Constitution and a few days later, on December 7, voted to ratify the document, making Delaware the first US state. Since 1933, that date has been celebrated as Delaware Day. In January 1790, delegates met again to approve the Bill of Rights.

A ROUND FOR THE HISTORY BOOKS

WHAT: Site of the Golden Fleece Tavern

WHERE: Northeast corner of The Green at State Street, Dover, DE

COST: Free

PRO TIP: First State Heritage Park offers regular walking tours of The Green with interpreters telling the stories of the different buildings that surround it.

A meeting of 30 delegates at this site on Dover's historic Green in 1787 led to Delaware becoming the First State. Photo by Dan Shortridge

The original Golden Fleece building was demolished in the 1830s and replaced by the Capital Hotel. The hotel closed in 1920, and was later renovated to better fit in with the other historic buildings on the Green by Henry and Mabel Lloyd Ridgley. Their grandson had ambitions to open a tavern there, but today an art gallery occupies the street level space.

There's a bar/restaurant called the Golden Fleece Tavern, which opened in 2019, just a few blocks away from the historic site on Loockerman Street. You have to be over 21 to enter.

THE KILLER'S CRANIUM

What's the story behind the skull of the "wickedest woman in America"?

The name of Patty Cannon has largely dwindled into history, but for a time she had a reputation as a cold-blooded killer and kidnapper.

While details of her life and crimes are sketchy and vague—tall tales mixed with unattributed early newspaper accounts—what emerges from a period in the late 1700s–early 1800s is a portrait of one of the nation's first serial killers.

Her gang, which operated along the Delaware-Maryland border near Seaford and Reliance, kidnapped free Black people and those who had escaped from bondage, selling them into slavery in the South. The crew was eventually busted up and Cannon brought into custody in 1829, when she was indicted after the three bodies were found on a piece of land she owned in Delaware.

Cannon was born around 1760 and died in jail in 1829, awaiting trial; rumor has it that she poisoned herself. Her body was buried in a pauper's grave in Georgetown—and therein lies additional mystery.

For decades, her skull—or what is believed to be her skull—floated around Delaware, hanging on a nail in the barn of a

Perhaps because of the notoriety, a neighborhood outside Seaford bears the name Patty Cannon Estates. "She was the Al Capone of this era," the developer of the community once told a local newspaper. "I've often wondered why no one made a movie of her."

An older historic marker sits just across the border in Maryland. Photo courtesy of the Delaware Public Archives

courthouse employee, and later put on display in the public library in Dover, the state capital, each Halloween. When the library moved, it was loaned to the Smithsonian for further study.

Not everyone is convinced of the skull's authenticity, including local historian Jim Bowden, who grew up in the Seaford area. He and others have located a descendant of Cannon's for a future DNA test to determine whether it actually is hers.

CANNON HISTORIC MARKER

WHAT: Historic marker dedicated to the victims

WHERE: At the Delaware and Maryland border near Seaford, at the intersection of Stein Highway and Line Road. The marker is located on the north side of the road.

COST: Free

PRO TIP: Just across the border, the state of Maryland has erected a historic marker at what was once believed to have been the site of Cannon's house.

MACHINERY MAN

What early American genius invented the water-powered mill?

The Thomas Edison of the Revolutionary era, Oliver Evans, was a mechanical genius who was constantly creating and experimenting with new technology.

Born in 1755 in Newport, in northern Delaware, Evans's legacy is inextricably linked to the transformation of milling, which was then a laborious process to turn wheat into flour. After working in a grain mill, he built one on his family's property in Delaware with two of his brothers.

Evans's efforts and ingenuity led to the creation of a production-line system churning out 300 bushels of flour each hour, using water wheels instead of muscle power. With an Evans mill, one worker could do the job of five. Evans's integration of five separate machines becomes even more innovative when one considers this was more than 100 years prior to Henry Ford's assembly line. Evans eventually licensed the milling system to more than 100 customers, including George Washington and Thomas Jefferson. His works included two books that helped spread the gospel of his new creations, *The Young Mill-Wright and Miller's Guide* and *The Young Steam Engineers' Guide*.

OLIVER EVANS HISTORIC MARKER

WHAT: A Delaware historic marker commemorating the life of Oliver Evans

WHERE: At Bicentennial Memorial Park in Evans' birthplace of Newport, at the intersection of Market Street, St. James Church Road, and Augustine Avenue.

COST: Free

PRO TIP: Far from his family home in Delaware, Evans is buried at Trinity Church Cemetery and Mausoleum in New York City.

The remains of a three-story Evans mill are visible at the Howell Mill site at Brecknock County Park near Camden. Built around 1812, the mill dam was washed away in 1928 by a storm and the building was demolished during a WWII scrap drive. Photo by Dan Shortridge

Evans continued his inventions—creating new ovens, lights, firearms, and steamboats, among others. Unfortunately, many of those innovations were borrowed or stolen by others, and he spent much time in legal battles. Known for a tough exterior, he also experienced depression during his lifetime. He died in 1819, three years after his wife, Sarah, and is buried in New York City.

Oliver Evans was also known for his work with steam engines. He built a portable engine that could run a wagon from Lancaster, Pennsylvania, to Philadelphia in a third less time.

QUARANTINE AT THE CAPE

What Delaware location served as a quarantine center for immigrants for three decades?

Today, thanks to COVID, we're all familiar with the word "quarantine"—isolating potentially sick people from contact with healthy ones to halt the spread of disease.

During the 1800s, however, quarantines were used to protect the American continent from a host of other deadly diseases, such as smallpox or cholera, that might be brought here by immigrants. In 1878, the National Quarantine Act led to the creation of stations around the nation that would screen, immunize, and hold people immigrating to the United States, including the Delaware Breakwater Quarantine Station in Delaware.

Located at what is now Cape Henlopen State Park, the station was the point of entry for all ships going to Wilmington and Philadelphia. When it opened in 1885, it held a home for a surgeon, kitchen, shed, and hospital with six beds. The station must have had somewhat of a bleak atmosphere, with 41 acres of mostly sand and a handful of trees—a far cry from the lush piney forests at the state park today.

DELAWARE BREAKWATER QUARANTINE STATION

WHAT: The former site of the quarantine station

WHERE: Cape Henlopen State Park, 15099 Cape Henlopen Drive, Lewes, DE

COST: Park entrance fees are in effect from May 1 to November 30 each year; see destateparks.com for current rates.

PRO TIP: While you're here, visit the park's other historical attraction, Fort Miles.

Left: *A home was built for the surgeon at the quarantine station. Photos courtesy of Delaware State Parks*

Right: *Immigrants being processed through the station by health workers.*

All ships carrying immigrants and any needing quarantine would drop anchor and be inspected by a doctor from the station. Anyone found to be sick would be taken back to the station and their clothing fumigated; the ship would stay off the coast for up to 12 weeks to guard against new cases of the disease.

With a surge of immigration in the 1890s, the station grew to add separate sections for men and women plus amenities such as sewers, bathhouses, a boathouse, and a building for laundry— as well as a crematorium and a graveyard for those who did not survive their journey.

With the coming of the Great War, the processing of immigrants halted as the US Navy took the station over as a base in 1917. All the buildings were removed by 1931, with the only physical remnants today being the foundation of the surgeon's house.

Handling up to eight ships per day, the station saw about 200,000 immigrants during its years in operation. Fewer than 5 percent of ships carried patients with communicable diseases.

INDIANA JONES'S WAREHOUSE

Why does the First State have a secret warehouse of treasured artifacts?

What do a microwave from the 1970s, "1" license plates used by former Delaware governors, portraits of famous Delawareans, and an unopened bottle of champagne from America's Bicentennial have in common?

They're all among the more than 90,000 objects in the historic collection of the Delaware Division of Historic and Cultural Affairs. Along with the more than four million pieces in the state's archeological collection, they're preserved, restored, and housed in a nondescript warehouse near downtown Dover.

While visitors aren't allowed inside that space, some objects from the collection—which also includes spinning wheels, statues and pieces of the *DeBraak*, a British warship that capsized off the Delaware coast in 1798—are on display at museums across the state, along with universities, office buildings and even at Woodburn, the official residence of Delaware's governor.

State agencies, colleges, and public officials can participate in a loan program with the Division. Some ask staff there to

COLLECTION HISTORY

WHAT: The Historic Collection of the Delaware Division of Historic and Cultural Affairs

WHERE: The full collection is not publicly accessible but you can see artifacts from it at locations across the state including the Delaware Public Archives, Legislative Hall, and Woodburn, the governor's residence, all located within blocks of each other in downtown Dover.

COST: Varies

PRO TIP: The Delaware Public Archives, Woodburn, and Legislative Hall are all free to visit, but you may need to make an appointment.

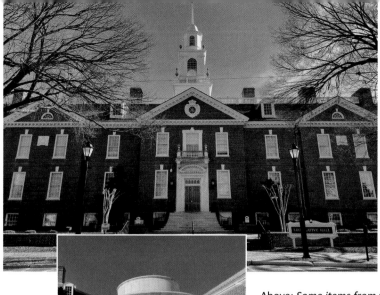

Above: *Some items from the warehouse are on display in Legislative Hall, where the General Assembly meets. Photos by Dan Shortridge*

Inset: *The Delaware Public Archives has artifacts and items on display from Delaware's history.*

choose pieces for them to brighten up utilitarian spaces, or add a little history to plain white walls. But others opt to come out to the warehouse and choose something that fits their color scheme, taste, or interests.

One of the recent acquisitions for the collection was a face mask and T-shirt featuring quotes from Dr. Martin Luther King Jr., which were worn by their creator during a Black Lives Matter protest on May 30, 2020, in Wilmington. The creator and a friend later sold copies of the mask and shirt and donated the proceeds to two nonprofit social justice and educational organizations.

One of the most unique pieces of the state's collection is a section of the hull of the DeBraak. It's kept at a conservation facility at Cape Henlopen State Park.

THE DELAWARE WORLD OF WAYNE

Where can you re-create a scene from an iconic movie from the 1990s?

Compared to hotspots like New York or Los Angeles, Delaware's contributions to the world of pop culture are few—but they're definitely memorable.

Take the First State's appearance in the 1992 hit movie *Wayne's World*, which was inspired by Mike Myers's and Dana Carvey's *Saturday Night Live* sketch about two rock-music fans who have a public-access TV show.

Delaware shows up in a scene where Wayne and Garth try out a green screen that allows them to "travel through time and space." After stops in New York, Hawaii, and Texas, the hosts ably come up with stories about their imaginary exploits seeing a Broadway show or riding a bronco. Then, a photo of the Indian River Inlet Bridge in southern Delaware flashes on screen and all a flummoxed Wayne can think of to say is "Hi. I'm in . . . Delaware."

Re-creating this scene during a trip to the Delaware beaches is pretty easy and it also shows that Wayne and Garth really don't give the First State's tourism appeal enough credit. The bridge spans the Indian River Bay between Dewey Beach and Bethany Beach. It was first built in 1934 and

HAVE A WAYNE'S WORLD MOMENT

WHAT: Visit the Indian River Inlet Bridge, which appears in a famous scene from the movie

WHERE: Delaware Rt. 1 between Dewey Beach and Bethany Beach

COST: Free

PRO TIP: Delaware Seashore State Park, immediately to the west of the northbound span, is home to Big Chill Beach Club, the perfect spot for a drink or a snack after you hike or bike the bridge.

The old Indian River Inlet Bridge, as seen in Wayne's World, *viewed from the air. Photo courtesy of the Delaware Department of Transportation*

has been replaced multiple times, most recently in 2012. While the bridge you'll see today isn't the same one shown in Wayne's World, the current span includes access lanes for cars, bikes, and pedestrians and passes over Delaware Seashore State Park.

Keep an eye on the Delaware State Parks website before you visit: the parks occasionally host guided hikes over the bridge with an interpreter.

One of Delaware's other star turns was in the 2003–2005 series Joan of Arcadia. Although the Girardi family lived in Maryland, the skyline shots of the fictional Arcadia are actually downtown Wilmington.

HONOR AND RESPECT

How does this unique Air Force operation care for America's fallen service members?

For nearly seven decades, Delaware has performed the most solemn of services for military dead.

Located at Dover Air Force Base is the largest US military mortuary, which handles the remains of all fallen service members and Defense Department civilian employees overseas. It also assists with incidents involving large numbers of fatalities at home.

The mortuary has handled the remains of the 913 dead from Jim Jones's cult in Guyana, of 188 people killed at the Pentagon on September 11, 2001, and the remains of the Space Shuttle Columbia's crew. It's also received bodies from the 1983 US Marine barracks bombing in Beirut, the mass shooting at Fort Hood, and the "Black Hawk Down" deaths in Somalia.

"We do the behind-the-scenes stuff that nobody wants to think about," said Army Sgt. 1st Class Nicole McMinamin.

The 85-member staff handles remains through a precise process. They are examined and scanned for unexploded ordnance. Personal items are catalogued. The service members' remains are photographed and weighed, X-rays are taken, and dental records, DNA, and fingerprints are analyzed. Autopsies are conducted, and the bodies are all embalmed for their trip home. Staff also prepare each body in their service branch's dress uniform, complete with all decorations and awards.

HONOR AND RESPECT

WHAT: US Air Force Mortuary Affairs Operations

WHERE: Dover Air Force Base, 331 Main Gateway, Dover, DE

COST: n/a

PRO TIP: The mortuary operations and dignified transfers are not open to the public.

Top Left: *Transfer cases carrying the remains of service members who died in Kabul, Afghanistan, line the inside of a C-17 Globemaster II at Dover Air Force Base. Photos courtesy of the US Air Force/Jason Minto*

Top Right: *A US Navy team transfers the remains of a Navy hospitalman as President Biden and the First Lady salute at Dover Air Force Base.*

Bottom Left: *A US Marine Corps team transfers the remains of a Marine sergeant.*

The base also conducts dignified transfers for every service member killed overseas. Teams from the specific branch move the transfer cases of remains from the aircraft to vehicles, which go directly to the mortuary.

The joint service staff is highly attentive to the needs of family members who may be on hand. "They just lost the one person that meant the world to them and you never know how they're going to cope with that fact," said Army Sgt. 1st Class William Carson. "We just try to be as respectful as we possibly can."

The heart of the mortuary, run by Air Force Mortuary Affairs Operations, is the Charles C. Carson Center for Mortuary Affairs, named after a civilian mortician who led the mortuary for 27 years.

ALONG THE BORDER

What are the stones that separate Maryland from Delaware?

On a back road outside of Dover, cars whiz by a small stone monument set back off the road.

The stone is a lasting monument of the Mason-Dixon Line—most famous for creating a divider between the North and South. In Delaware, it cuts between the east and the west. The First State is the only state that is actually east of the line.

Charles Mason and Jeremiah Dixon were commissioned in 1763 to settle a boundary fracas between the Penn family and the Calverts, who had overlapping deeds from the British crown. They started their 233-mile journey near what is now Delmar, using a marker called Middle Point.

They surveyed through thick forests and forded creeks to lay out the line, accompanied by a crew that carried chains and tents, and other workers who chopped down trees so the surveyors could make their sightings—39 people in all, according to Mason's journal.

It seems as though Mason-Dixon markers are everywhere in Delaware. There's one inside a locked pavilion in Delmar (once recovered by police after vandals ripped it out of the ground with a chain and a car).

One marker sits outside of Newark underneath a manhole cover—the original site had become a highway turn lane,

Mason and Dixon's final bill for the costs of their journeys was 3,500 British pounds—about 604,000 pounds today, or $823,000 US dollars.

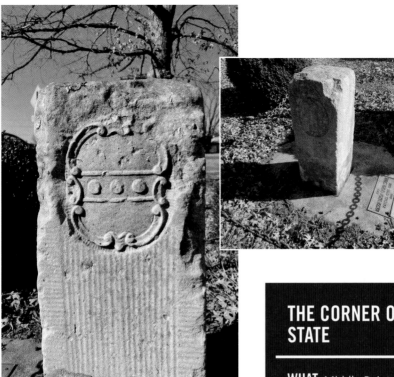

Left: *This Mason-Dixon marker near Marydel was moved away from the road in 1968. Photos by Dan Shortridge*

Right: *This Mason-Dixon crownstone near Marydel was put on display by Maryland for the 1904 St. Louis World's Fair and then at the Annapolis statehouse for 50 years, and was returned in 1954.*

THE CORNER OF THE STATE

WHAT: Middle Point, the Mason-Dixon monument located at the southwest corner of Delaware

WHERE: Along Delaware Rt. 54, about 6 miles west of Delmar

COST: Free

PRO TIP: The locked pavilion includes two other markers from colonial days, plus a plain stone put there by a local resident who thought it looked like the official markers.

so it was lowered underneath the road's surface. Three were reportedly painted yellow to keep hunters from going across the border. And one near Seaford was paved over in 1951, later to be dug out and placed nearby.

DESEGREGATION DECISION

How did two Delaware cases help lead to the landmark *Brown v. Board of Education* ruling?

Delaware's racist tradition of segregated "colored" schools (see Separate Schools, page 38), despite initial funding from a du Pont, meant that Black children were forced into largely substandard educations.

Black parents and advocates fought for their children to receive the same schooling as their White counterparts, and took that fight to the courts. Two cases in the First State were eventually consolidated into the legal arguments in *Brown v. Board of Education*, ruled on by the US Supreme Court in 1954.

Bulah v. Gebhart involved school officials' refusal to take a Black child on a Whites-only bus to Hockessin Colored School #107, and *Belton v. Gebhart* argued that Black children should be able to attend Claymont High School close to their homes, instead of the all-Black Howard High School farther away.

The cases were filed in 1951 by civil-rights attorney Louis Redding, the first Black lawyer in Delaware. He had previously taken on and beaten the University of Delaware over segregation.

In April 1952, Delaware Chancery Court Chancellor Collins Seitz ruled in favor of both plaintiffs, declaring that segregated

Civil-rights attorney Louis Redding, who passed away in 1998, has a middle school and state office building named after him. Chancellor Collins Seitz Sr.'s son, Collins Seitz Jr., is the chief justice of the Delaware Supreme Court.

Howard High School, seen during the days of segregation in 1936. Photo courtesy of the Delaware Public Archives

DESEGREGATION DECISION

schools were inherently unequal. "The separate facilities and opportunities afforded these plaintiffs, and those similarly situated, are not equal to those offered white children," Seitz wrote.

The state appealed, and the case landed before the US high court. It took years after that 1954 decision for full desegregation to occur in Delaware, however.

Howard High School became the Howard Career Center in 1975, focusing on vocational-technical programs. It became part of the New Castle County

WHAT: Two all-Black schools at the center of pivotal desegregation rulings in Delaware

WHERE: Howard High School, 401 E. 12th St., Wilmington, DE; Hockessin Colored School #107, 4266 Millcreek Rd., Hockessin, DE

COST: n/a

PRO TIP: Find more information and support redevelopment efforts from the Friends of Hockessin Colored School at hockessincoloredschool107.org.

Vocational Technical School District, and its name was changed to Howard High School of Technology in the 1990s.

Hockessin Colored School #107 closed in 1959. In 2012, it was rescued from a foreclosure sale by a group of friends and alumni, and in 2020 it became the newest New Castle County park site. It is being redeveloped into a center for educational enrichment, equity, and diversity training, and other uses.

To the First State's shame, it was not until 1995—41 years after *Brown*—that state lawmakers got around to removing the official stamp of segregation from the state Constitution, voting to strike language stating that "separate schools for white and colored children shall be maintained."

HISTORY AND NATURE

Which green space was both a stop on the Underground Railroad and a former landfill?

Hunn Nature Park lacks a lot of the bells and whistles of the other green spaces in the Kent County parks system: there are no playgrounds, no ball fields, and no bathrooms. But it more than makes up for the lack of amenities with a fascinating history that dates all the way back to the 18th century.

The 173-acre park gets its name from the Hunn family, who were Quaker landowners and active abolitionists. Their home, which still stands, was called Wildcat Manor; patriarch John Hunn was a "stationmaster" on the Underground Railroad and operated the site as a link for slaves escaping to freedom in the North (one of his sons, John Hunn Jr., would later become governor of Delaware).

After the Civil War, freed slaves settled on the property in what became known as "Hunn Town." There are vine-covered hand pumps along the trails that are remnants from that time. But by the mid-20th century, part of what is today the park was actually used as a landfill. It was cleaned up in the 1980s and 1990s. In the early 2000s the county bought the site with an eye to develop it into a park that could also become part of the St. Jones Greenway, which will connect downtown Dover to the Delaware Bay.

Hunn Nature Park's "racetrack pond" path also has a view of Lebanon Landing, one of Dover's first commercial ports. It was also a stop for Philadelphia-bound ships in the 18th and 19th centuries.

Left: *Several bridges help create a loop trail around a tidal basin. Photos by Rachel Kipp*

Right: *The Hunns' ancestral home, known as Wildcat Manor, was a station on the Underground Railroad.*

Volunteers and Kent County Parks employees spent years cleaning up the park, clearing trails, planting trees, and clearing out invasive non-native plants. Today, the park's two primary hikes—a one-mile in-and-back trail and a half-mile loop around a tidal basin—are a tranquil escape that offers scenery of meadows, forest, and wetlands all year round.

A PEEK INTO THE PAST

WHAT: Hunn Nature Park, at the site of a former stop on the Underground Railroad

WHERE: 1624 Sorghum Mill Rd., Dover, DE

COST: Free

PRO TIP: Like all Kent County Parks, Hunn Nature Park closes at sunset, which can be as early as 5 p.m. in winter.

A BEACH'S BOUNTY

How did a newspaper reporter walking her dog uncover a treasure trove of underwater artifacts?

The late longtime Delaware reporter Molly Murray was well known for her encyclopedic knowledge of local history and fascinating environmental facts. Living just steps from the beach in Lewes, she loved to spend time exploring the coast and communing with the ocean and bay.

That's how, in 2004, she was one of the first to discover a cache of 250-year-old artifacts from the seabed.

Former state preservation expert Dan Griffith recalled the day when Murray walked up after a presentation he'd done, carrying a shoebox of items from her beachcombing.

"I said, 'These are pretty cool, Molly. Where did you get that?' And then I immediately sent a crew out to report back to me," Griffith told a magazine reporter later.

What Murray had found were artifacts from a hitherto unknown shipwreck, beginning to wash up by the thousands.

Initially, it was suspected that the treasures may have come from the first Dutch settlement in Delaware, a village known as Swanendael. It turned out that a beach replenishment project, dredging sand to pump it back onto the beach, had apparently sliced through the ship's wreckage and revealed history, washing up on the beach at Roosevelt Inlet.

BEACH'S BOUNTY

WHAT: Artifacts from a 1774 shipwreck

WHERE: On display in the "Rediscovery through Recovery" exhibit at the Zwaanendael Museum, 102 Kings Highway, Lewes, DE

COST: Free

PRO TIP: Visit history.delaware.gov/zwaanendael-museum/ for museum hours and tours.

Left: *The items began washing up on the beach near Roosevelt Inlet in Lewes. Photo by Dan Shortridge*

Inset: *A glass linen-smoother was one of the artifacts uncovered by the beach replenishment project. Photo courtesy of the Delaware Division of Historical and Cultural Affairs*

"The dredge basically took part of the archeological wreck through a blender and threw it a mile and a half. Then bulldozers spread it all over the beach," Griffith explained.

The site was located a year later, with evidence indicating it was a merchant ship that foundered in 1774. Artifacts that survived 230 years submerged in the deep included glass bottles, stoneware, glazed earthenware, and shoe buckles.

The recovery effort involved dozens of volunteers sorting through sand that had been pumped ashore to pick out clothing buckles, pot pieces, and glass and ceramic artifacts.

POET IN THE PARK

Why does this town have a seated statue of the author of "Paradise Lost"?

Like many communities in the early days of the new nation, the town on the Broadkill River had several names: Upper Landing, Conwell Landing, Osburn's Landing, Head-of-the-Broadkill, and Head of Broadkiln.

But in 1807, a group of local citizens petitioned the state legislature to change the town's name to the simpler, plainer "Milton."

Today, no one quite knows why. Some theorize that it came from the grist mills that once dotted the area. (See also the southern towns of Milford and Millsboro.)

But for many residents, the story that their town was named after the famed English poet and author John Milton (1608–1674) was simply too good to pass up. Best known for his epic *Paradise Lost*, Milton was also an activist for a free press.

That version of the naming story gathered traction over the years, and in 2008, the citizenry erected a piece of public art cementing the poet's place in their history. They raised funds to commission and install a life-sized bronze statue of John Milton, placed on a bench in Mill Park. Today, the statue is occasionally accoutered in scarves and hats for the weather by well-meaning friends.

At the dedication ceremony for the statue, British Consul Oliver St. Clair Franklin spoke and brought greetings from the royal family.

The John Milton statue is occasionally decorated with hats, scarves, or other ornamentation. Photo by Dan Shortridge

POET IN THE PARK

WHAT: A statue of the English poet and author John Milton

WHERE: 114 Mulberry St., Milton, DE

COST: Free

PRO TIP: While you're in town, catch a performance at the historic Milton Theatre.

Milton's broader history is the story of several economic booms and busts. During its first two centuries, the town was known for shipbuilding, then canning, then button-making, brick manufacturing, and holly wreath production. Today, it's a quiet community off the beaten path, home to the famed Dogfish Head brewery.

COOKIN' CHICKEN

What was the world's largest frying pan used for?

What would it take to cook about 200 chickens at the same time?

Delawareans know.

For six decades, they and their neighbors in Maryland and Virginia enjoyed the output of the world's largest frying pan—definitely the world's largest chicken frying pan, for certain.

Approximately the size of a medium trampoline (10 feet in diameter) and weighing about as much as a green anaconda (650 pounds), the frying pan was put into action each year at the Delmarva Chicken Festival, celebrating one of the region's most important industries (see "Cluck, Cluck, Oops," page 42).

The first pan actually made its debut in 1950, at the festival's third year. Crafted by the Mumford Sheet Metal Works of Selbyville, the original pan is now on display at the Marvel

GIANT FRYING PAN

WHAT: The world's largest frying pan

WHERE: On display at the Marvel Carriage Museum, 510 S. Bedford St., Georgetown, DE

COST: Free

PRO TIP: The museum is staffed by volunteers, so call ahead for details on hours: 302-855-9660.

Other frying pans purport to be the world's largest—there are pretenders in Iowa, Washington state, North Carolina, and others. A New York newspaper once declared Delaware's to be "perhaps the least picturesque." We know they're just jealous.

This frying pan could hold 800 chicken quarters at a time. Photo courtesy of the Delaware Public Archives

Carriage Museum in Georgetown. Used for 38 years, it cooked an estimated 100 tons of chicken over the decades.

Its successor could cook 800 chicken quarters at the same time in 180 gallons of oil. The cooks would use long-handled metal rake-like devices to carefully stir up the chicken and keep it from burning; the pan itself was set on a sturdy base of concrete blocks. It used about 150 gallons of gas over two days.

The replacement pan was purchased by a local company known for its fried chicken. The Delmarva Chicken Festival was last held in 2014, after a 65-year run.

FREEDOM TO SHOP

How did this shopping center come to bear a "revolutionary" design?

Visitors to this North Wilmington shopping center with a historic flair may think they weren't listening closely in civics class: Isn't Independence Hall in Philadelphia?

Indeed, our founding fathers debated and adopted the Declaration of Independence and US Constitution 30 miles up the road in the City of Brotherly Love. But it's fitting that sales tax-free Delaware is the home of Independence Mall, with a center building designed to look exactly like the famous historic site.

Emilio Capaldi, a builder with an affinity for American history, developed the unusual shopping center. According to the center's website, Capaldi told a reporter when Independence *Mall* opened in 1964 that most shopping centers "leave no impression on you after you leave them. They're sort of long, gray lines. . . . That's why I wanted to build something that adds to the overall appearance of my city."

The U-shaped shopping center has 25 first floor shops and 25 upper-floor spaces for offices. A painting of Capaldi (painted by his daughter, who now owns the center) hangs in the foyer of the Independence Hall replica building. Employees of the Melting Pot, the space's longtime tenant, have been known to joke with curious customers that our founding fathers were fondue fans.

The rest of the Independence Mall is set up to look like Philadelphia's Old City neighborhood—keep an eye out for the Betsy Ross House and Carpenter's Hall.

The life-sized replica of the Liberty Bell will be returning to an outdoor location on the property at Independence Mall. Photo by Rachel Kipp

SHOP (OR DINE) LIKE IT'S 1776

WHAT: Independence Mall, a shopping center that is a replica of Independence Hall in Philadelphia

WHERE: 1601 Concord Pike (Rt. 202), Suite 22, Wilmington, DE

COST: Free

PRO TIP: Keep an eye out for the faux historic plaques outside of the center's replica buildings.

Until a few years ago, the foyer also featured a replica Liberty Bell, which Capaldi's grandson says was cast from the real one in Philadelphia—"the only difference is the [replica's] crack is fake," and Emilio Capaldi's signature is at the bottom, Joe Capaldi says. The bell had to be moved because there was no longer room for it when an elevator was constructed in the building. But it's been restored, cleaned, and polished, and plans are to bring it back in an outdoor kiosk on the property.

BEES ON WHEELS

Why do up to 240 million bees visit Delaware each year?

We all know that bees make honey. But what many people still don't understand is their vital role in growing other crops as well.

Bees are critical to pollinating many fruits and vegetables. That includes crops that keep Delaware farmers thriving, with fields and orchards bearing such bounty as watermelon, apples, cucumbers, blueberries, strawberries, pumpkins, and cantaloupes.

Delaware has about 270 registered beekeepers maintaining up to 3,000 hives—not enough to meet the needs. To bolster the local population, the First State's farmers temporarily import even more bees—about 3,000 colonies every season.

"The business is on wheels," the state's apiarist once told a reporter. "These people take their hives all over to pollinate crops."

The guest worker bees are mainly imported from nearby states—Maryland, Virginia, Pennsylvania, and New Jersey—

BUSY, BUSY BEES

WHAT: The Delaware Beekeepers Association holds Beekeeping 101 workshops

WHERE: Visit www.delawarebeekeepers.com for details

COST: Varies

PRO TIP: Beehives can also be seen in action during the growing season in wooden boxes stacked in farm fields across the state.

It takes up to 1,000 grains of pollen to pollinate the blossom of just one watermelon so it grows properly, or up to four trips by the bees.

Delaware imports about 3,000 bee colonies every year to help pollinate its fruit and vegetable crops. Photo courtesy of the Delaware Department of Agriculture

where about 10 commercial apiaries offer the service to farmers. The cost can add up, with pollination being about 3 to 5 percent of a farmer's growing costs.

With bee populations nationwide beset by disease, it can be a struggle for some farmers to keep up with the competition. One year, for example, a Dover beekeeper lost 80 percent of his beehives and had to pull some on loan from a neighboring state. Another year, Delaware benefited from cutbacks in New Jersey cranberry production, which freed up bees to come here.

ONLY A DOG CAN HEAR

Why is this music-focused museum full of dog art?

The Johnson Victrola Museum in downtown Dover is dedicated to the history of recorded music, including the life of Eldridge Johnson, a Wilmington native who co-founded the Victor Talking Machine Company in 1901. Johnson also invented a spring motor that was used to power a phonograph turntable, leading to the Victrola becoming a household staple.

But the museum also has a room full of statues and pictures of dogs—actually, just one dog in particular. Like Johnson, the terrier named Nipper played a key role in music history. The real Nipper lived in England in the late 1800s and was the subject of a painting where he is depicted listening to a phonograph. Eventually, the painting became a trademark for the Gramophone Company in London, and then was later acquired by Johnson's company, Victor. Through Johnson's marketing efforts, the Company in London, and then was later acquired by Johnson's company, Victor. Through Johnson's marketing efforts, the

MEET "HIS MASTER'S VOICE"

WHAT: Johnson Victrola Museum

WHERE: 375 S. New St., Dover, DE

COST: Free

PRO TIP: Check the hours before you go—the museum is only for 45-minute self-guided tours on Wednesdays through Sundays during scheduled tour times, which are 10 a.m., 11 a.m., 1 p.m., and 2 p.m. To book your tour, please call the museum at 302-739-3262.

The real Nipper's final resting place is in Kingston upon Thames in England. An alley in the town center was also renamed in honor of the famous canine.

A marketing campaign made Nipper a multimedia star of his age. Photo courtesy of the Delaware Public Archives

public's affection for Victrolas extended to the company's canine pitchman and Nipper became a collectible, with his image turned into stuffed animals, salt and pepper shakers, wall decor, and more.

You can see just a sampling of the various homages to Nipper at the museum, along with early record players of all sizes, shapes, and colors.

THE PRINTED PAGE

Why are this small publisher and bookshop obsessed with books about books?

If you're reading this, then you probably enjoy books.

But it's doubtful you love them quite as much as Robert Fleck Jr. did.

Inspired by his love for the printed page, Fleck founded a highly specialized bookshop and publishing company—focused on books about books.

Fleck founded Oak Knoll's bookstore in 1976 and the publishing arm in 1978 after departing a career in chemical engineering.

"There were a lot of people then in the field of modern literature, but no one was specializing in the book arts field, books about books," he recalled in the 1990s. "So it was a conscious business decision to get into that field."

Oak Knoll's 27,000-book inventory includes titles on design, graphic arts, libraries, papermaking, calligraphy, and bookbinding, among plenty of other topics. The company co-publishes some books with scholarly institutions and private libraries.

In 1998, Oak Knoll moved down the block in historic New Castle—a short distance, but a daunting venture for a business with 30,000 books. Workers ordered 4,400 packing boxes and ran out, and a crane had to lift the books up through a window on the third floor of the 1879 building.

THE PRINTED PAGE

WHAT: Oak Knoll Books and Press

WHERE: 310 Delaware St., New Castle, DE

COST: Free to visit, but bring your card or cash in case you spot a good read!

PRO TIP: Visit www.oakknoll.com or call ahead, 302-328-7232, to check on hours of operation.

Oak Knoll Books is the perfect place to satisfy your inner bibliophile. Photo by Rachel Kipp

The company also holds an annual book festival, Oak Knoll Fest. Postponed in 2020 due to the COVID-19 pandemic, it was held virtually in 2021.

Fleck took great pride in his personal collection of Delaware books and publications, numbering in the thousands. He was a leader in the bookselling and book arts field. Notably, Fleck was ahead of his time in selling online, launching the Oak Knoll website in the late 1990s. During the first two years, online sales rose to 15 percent of his business. "A lot of people who are finding me didn't know I existed," Fleck recalled in a 1999 interview. "All of a sudden, the out-of-print book world is becoming open to the public."

In 2016, he passed away and left the business to his son, Robert Fleck III, who heads the antiquarian books arm and is the face of the company.

Perhaps the least surprising title from Oak Knoll's publishing arm is the 2008 volume *Books About Books*. It's a history of Oak Knoll itself, written by founder Robert Fleck, which includes the press's full bibliography.

THE UFO HOUSE

Why does this airport have its own ski chalet–which looks like a flying saucer?

No, the strange round building perched near the Eagle Crest Aerodrome airfield in Milton isn't a flying saucer.

Actually, the prefabricated structures were originally conceived by Finnish architect Matti Suuronen in 1968 as portable "ski chalets" that could be the solution to the world's housing shortage. But the design never quite caught on, and only about 100 were sold worldwide in the late 1960s and early 1970s.

The Milton Futuro House found its way to Delaware when local developer Joe Hudson became the distributor working with Suuronen's company in the early 1970s to try to sell the Futuro in Delaware and four other states. He had three models, one of which became his first office.

Hudson set up one of the models at one of his developments, the Villages of Five Points. He told a local newspaper that long lines of people would come to see the inside. Several residents contacted him asking about buying one of the houses to use as a guest quarters. Though he had several orders, Hudson was only able to sell three or four Futuros due to supply and delivery issues. Suuronen's company went out of business in the early 1970s.

Futuro Houses are relatively rare, but Delaware is actually home to two—the other one is a private home in Houston. The couple who call it home have lived there for more than 40 years.

Only about 100 of these ski chalets were ever sold. Photo by Rachel Kipp

HOUSE OF THE FUTURE

WHAT: A rare "Futuro House" at the Eagle Crest Aerodrome

WHERE: 29763 Eagle Crest Rd., Milton, DE

COST: Free

PRO TIP: The Milton area isn't hurting for unique homes— just a 10-minute drive away from the Futuro House is the "Steampunk Treehouse" on the campus of Dogfish Head Brewery.

The flying saucer-shaped houses are made of fiberglass-reinforced polyester plastic. Measuring 13 feet high and 26 feet in diameter and featuring 16 oval windows, the Futuro has a bedroom, a bathroom, a kitchen, a living room, and a fireplace. They cost $15,900.

Though the Futuro never gained mainstream popularity, it's gained a small but loyal following and has been the subject of books, articles, and art exhibits. The house in Milton has been used as rental property and Hudson says interested onlookers stop by almost daily to snap photos.

ACROSS THE BAY

Why is part of Delaware in New Jersey?

Here's something they didn't teach you in elementary-school geography class: while the Delaware River and Bay make up most of the border between Delaware and its neighbor to the north and east, there is a tiny part of the First State that actually shares a land border with New Jersey.

The story of the 580-acre piece of land near Pennsville, New Jersey, dates all the way back to before the Revolutionary War. When the border was being drawn for the Delaware colony, William Penn and former King of England Charles II agreed to draw a 12-mile circle around the city of New Castle. The circle extends all the way to what was then the low tide line of the Jersey shore.

The area now known to locals as "the Baja" was once a federally protected bird habitat called Killcohook National Wildlife Refuge. But over time, the US Army Corps of Engineers started dredging the river and depositing silt on the site, turning it into solid ground.

The land has been the subject of multiple court cases, with New Jersey unsuccessfully arguing that it should have ownership. There have also been challenges with police jurisdiction, since New Jersey needs to call the Delaware State Police to handle any incidents that come up.

SEE THE FIRST STATE IN THE GARDEN STATE

WHAT: "The Baja," a small piece of Delaware that's actually in New Jersey

WHERE: Near Pennsville, NJ, visible from Fort Mott State Park

COST: Free

PRO TIP: From late May through late September, you can take a half-mile ferry ride between Fort Delaware on Pea Patch Island in the First State and Fort Mott in New Jersey.

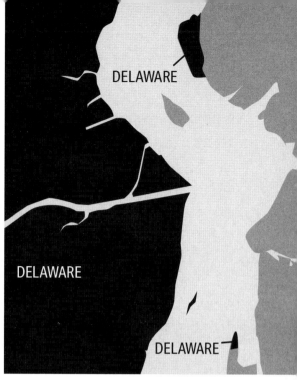

Left: *Viewed from historic Fort Mott, this small slice of Delaware is in the distance, just to the left of the tower. Photo courtesy of New Jersey Department of Environmental Protection*

Right: *Map by Hanna Manninen*

Today, "the Baja" is mostly blocked off by the Army Corps of Engineers but it is visible in the distance to visitors to New Jersey's Fort Mott State Park.

There's one more chunk of Delaware that's also in the Garden State: Delaware owns part of Artificial Island, an island in the Delaware Bay that is home to the Hope Creek Nuclear Power Plant.

A GUIDING LIGHT

What's the story behind the large red boat anchored along a canal?

It's hard to miss the big red boat floating in the Lewes and Rehoboth Canal when driving through town on your way to dinner or the beach. But while the former floating lighthouse is now a beloved Lewes landmark, decades ago, it was in danger of sinking due to neglect.

The *Overfalls* was one of 179 lightships built between 1820 and 1952 to help guide ships. Built in 1938, the *Overfalls* served stints in Long Island Sound, near Cape Cod and Boston Harbor before being donated to the Lewes Historical Society by the Coast Guard in 1972. Although the ship was never in service on the Delaware Bay, another lightship was from 1898 to 1960.

But the historical society struggled to preserve the ship and get it in shape to be open to the public. The organization even tried to sell the *Overfalls* until a group of volunteers decided to form a separate 501(c)3 group to focus on saving it.

Volunteers fixed rusted areas and peeling paint, removed dirt and grime, repaired holes, upgraded the ship's electrical system, and removed 28,000 pounds of pig-iron ballast from the ship's bilge. In 2010, they moved the *Overfalls* into a new slip created near Canalfront Park.

LIGHTSHIP OVERFALLS

WHAT: A decommissioned "floating lighthouse" now a floating museum near downtown Lewes

WHERE: 219 Pilottown Rd., Lewes, DE

COST: $5 for anyone age 15 and over

PRO TIP: The museum is open spring through late fall, but open days and hours change throughout the season. Off-season and group tours are available upon request.

The lightship Overfalls *is a local landmark in Lewes and host of the town's New Year's Anchor Drop. Photo by Rachel Kipp*

Today, visitors can tour the ship, which is now a national historic landmark, and learn more about maritime history. The *Overfalls* is also the place to be every December 31, when Lewes celebrates the New Year with a ceremonial Anchor Drop. In 2021 the *Overfalls* Foundation installed a webcam and weather station in the ship's crow's nest, taking it back to its roots as a resource for boaters and fishermen.

The *Overfalls* is next to Lewes Canalfront Park, which features a nautical-themed playground, green space, and, in the summertime, free concerts, exercise classes, and more.

A WEDGE ISSUE

Why were 800 acres of Delaware disputed territory until 1921?

It's called the Wedge, but the Sliver might be a better name for it. For more than 100 years, Delaware and Pennsylvania had a state-level feud over ownership of an 800-acre long, narrow section of land just west of the Delaware "curve."

The Wedge's existence stems from the 12-mile radius used to lay it all out back in the 1680s, with the arc drawn from a New Castle church. The curve of the circle did not connect neatly with the surveys done by Mason and Dixon (see Along the Border, page 70). An 1840s re-survey by the US Corps of Topographic Engineers gave the Wedge to Pennsylvania, but Delaware refused to acknowledge it.

In practice, the Wedge was governed by Delaware law during that time, although some sources say it was lawless territory. Eventually, in 1889, the two states got down to business and named a joint commission to tackle the dispute. Each state appointed members.

In the end, the commission awarded possession of the Wedge to Delaware. Pennsylvania signed off on the matter in 1897, but for some reason Delaware dragged its feet and didn't get around to approving it until 1921. Congress OK'd the resolution shortly thereafter.

A WEDGE ISSUE

WHAT: The Wedge

WHERE: A historic marker is located on New London Road outside of Newark, about a quarter-mile east of the state line.

COST: n/a

PRO TIP: There aren't many places to park near the marker and it's along a busy road, so be careful and cautious.

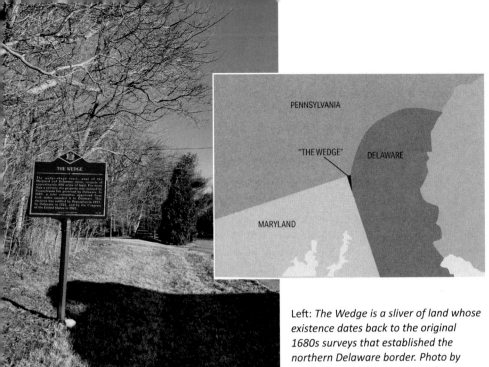

THE WEDGE

The wedge-shape track, west of the Maryland and Delaware curve, results of approximate 800 acres of land. For more than a century, the property was claimed by Pennsylvania but governed by Delaware. In 1889, a joint committee appointed from both states awarded it to Delaware. This decision was ratified by Pennsylvania 1897, by Delaware in 1921, and by the Congress of the United States in 1921.

PENNSYLVANIA

"THE WEDGE"   DELAWARE

MARYLAND

Left: *The Wedge is a sliver of land whose existence dates back to the original 1680s surveys that established the northern Delaware border. Photo by Rachel Kipp*

Right: *Map by Hanna Manninen*

In 2021, New Castle County made an April Fools' joke that it had ceded the Wedge back to the Keystone State "per the terms of our 100-year rental agreement with Pennsylvania." The county government tweeted: "Best of luck to all the former First Countians living there."

What is now Delaware was originally held by English charter by the Calvert family. The land was later given to William Penn by James, the Duke of York, to settle a debt owed by the Crown.

RAINBOW OVER REHOBOTH

How did a sleepy Methodist resort transform into an LGBTQ+ destination?

Rehoboth Beach has its roots as a Methodist meeting camp town in the 1870s. But modern-day Rehoboth is centered in a thriving gay community that has come into its own over the last three decades.

Rehoboth is known as the "Nation's Summer Capital" because of the number of Washington, DC residents who visit during the season. Among their numbers were a number of gay men who enjoyed the resort atmosphere and kept coming back.

By the 1950s and 1960s, the Pink Pony Bar and several gay-friendly guest houses catered to the community. In the 1970s, two dance clubs opened, with several hundred gay men enjoying the age of disco on some weekends. In the 1970s and '80s, gay and lesbian restaurants came of age with the opening of the Back Porch Restaurant and the Blue Moon. By 1981, there were three gay bars and three guest houses in the area.

It wasn't all smooth sailing—far from it. In the mid-1980s, the town's mayor was called homophobic over his comments about "a gay problem." In the 1990s, there was increasing backlash: some residents boasted dog-whistle bumper stickers

REHOBOTH RAINBOW

WHAT: The CAMP Rehoboth office and community center, a focal point and information source for the gay community

WHERE: 37 Baltimore Ave., Rehoboth Beach, DE

COST: Free

PRO TIP: Stop in at Browseabout Books and pick up one or three of Fay Jacobs's books, packed with laughs and stories about life in Rehoboth.

Left: *The Blue Moon is an iconic local restaurant on Baltimore Avenue. Photos by Dan Shortridge*

Right: *CAMP Rehoboth organizes events and publishes information for the LGBTQ+ community.*

reading "Keep Rehoboth a Family Town," others fought a liquor license for a gay bar, and there were even horrific gay-bashing assaults.

In response, the community created CAMP Rehoboth, a community organization that became an unofficial chamber of commerce and visitors' center for LGBTQ+ visitors. Delaware soon approved hate-crimes legislation that the governor signed in front of the Rehoboth police station.

CAMP Rehoboth—"Creating a More Positive Rehoboth"—was founded by partners Murray Archibald and Steve Elkins; Elkins served as executive director for 25 years until his death in 2018, and Archibald was president and interim executive director.

For many years, an area known as Poodle Beach was a safe place for gays and lesbians to hang out on the sand. A historic marker for the site is in the works.

HONORING THE FALLEN

Where can you see a "rough draft" of a 9/11 memorial?

Those who encounter the giant figure with head in hands at the entrance to the Copeland Sculpture Garden at the Delaware Art Museum may wonder: Why does the figure look so sad?

The 10-foot-tall bronze sculpture was actually a "rough draft" for a much more intricate project by artist Tom Otterness: a memorial to the September 11, 2001, terrorist-attack victims. The memorial was to be made of copper, with eyes that dripped water into pools below. There were also plans for an elevator that would allow viewers to access an attached observation deck.

Delaware's *Crying Giant* is actually one of three: the other two are at the Kemper Museum of Contemporary Art in Kansas City, Missouri, and at the Scheveningen sculpture park in the Hague, Netherlands.

While the full memorial was never built, Otterness's sculpture lends a feeling of solemnity and wonder to the Delaware Art Museum's garden. The garden also features a sculpture by Domenico Mortellito of a figure protecting a child from pollution, and brightly colored abstract metal sculptures by Betty Gold, Joe Moss, David Stromeyer, and Isaac Witkin. There's

---

The Copeland sculpture garden also features a mural of peacock feathers by artist Laura Erickson that is part of the 13-stop Delaware Discoveries trail, which features interactive art in all three counties.

Other Crying Giant *sculptures are in Missouri and the Netherlands. Photo by Rachel Kipp*

also an 80-foot-wide labyrinth based on medieval manuscript drawings.

In the warmer months, the garden is used for outdoor movies, story walks, concerts, and more.

THE *CRYING GIANT* SCULPTURE

WHAT: Part of the sculpture garden at the Delaware Art Museum, the statue was a "rough draft" for a planned 9/11 memorial

WHERE: Delaware Art Museum, 2301 Kentmere Parkway, Wilmington, DE

COST: The sculpture garden is free to enter. Museum admission is $14 for adults, $7 for students, $6 for kids ages 7–18, and free for kids 6 and under.

PRO TIP: The museum is free on Sundays and 4–8 p.m. on Thursdays from April to December.

TREASURE TROVE

Why do treasure hunters search for Captain Kidd's booty in Delaware?

Fans of buccaneers well know the name Captain William Kidd. More than 300 years ago, while fleeing the British Royal Navy, the pirate Kidd anchored his ship in the Delaware Bay—and created a treasure-hunting legend lasting to this day.

In June 1699, Kidd sailed up to the future Delaware coast on board the sloop *Saint Antonia*, after a journey to the Indian Ocean. He had just come from the West Indies, where he'd learned that the British were after him.

While his ship was off the coast of what is now Lewes, a few local residents came aboard, guests of the Scottish-born captain, and reported back on his treasure—bringing some items back with them. "These men went constantly onboard him and brought ashore with them great quantities of East India goods," stated a report lodged today in the Maryland Archives.

After leaving Cape Henlopen, Kidd went to Boston and was promptly seized, hauled to London, tried, and killed. Local stories spread about the *Saint Antonia*'s haul, leading to a long tradition holding that Kidd had buried some of the treasure on Delaware's shores.

That tale was bolstered in 1890, when workers digging a foundation uncovered a blue stone buried five feet under the

KIDD'S TREASURE?

WHAT: Rumors about possible treasure hidden by Captain Kidd

WHERE: Cape Henlopen State Park is a likely option, 15099 Cape Henlopen Drive, Lewes, DE

COST: Varies by season; see destateparks.com/Beaches/CapeHenlopen for current fees.

PRO TIP: Bring your metal detector to stroll the beach, but don't start digging up the dunes. They're off-limits due to their role protecting the rest of the coastline.

No one alive today knows for sure if Captain Kidd's treasure lies along the long stretch of Atlantic beach. Photos by Dan Shortridge

sand. The rectangular rock was described as two feet thick and six feet long, with the letter "K" carved into one side.

Noted a Delaware newspaper in its account: "The fact that almost every sea port town on the Atlantic coast has a similar tradition respecting Kidd's treasure has not seemed to detract in the least from the strength and the blindness of faith locally reposed in this story."

There's no telling where Kidd hid his treasure, but that hasn't stopped hunters from hoping for years for a gold coin to turn up along Lewes Beach or in Cape Henlopen State Park.

A wealthy New Yorker, Kidd originally applied for a commission in the Royal Navy, but the Crown's agents needed a privateer instead to go after the pirates in the Red Sea.

HALL OF FAMER

What Delawarean had an astounding baseball career in the Negro Leagues?

Like many other Black baseball players during the dark days of segregation, William Julius "Judy" Johnson would have been a major-league star if he'd lived in later times.

As it was, his natural talents led him to a role as an ace third baseman and slugger in the Negro Leagues, playing from 1921 to 1937. He played for the Hillsdale Giants in the first Negro Leagues World Series in 1924, and was named MVP in 1929 by two major Black newspapers.

A year later, he was both a player and manager of the Homestead Grays, and in 1932 left the Grays (with many other players) for the Pittsburgh Crawfords, serving as team captain in 1935. Johnson played in more than 700 games, with 33 home runs and a .346 RBI.

Though born just over the southern border in Snow Hill, Maryland, Judy Johnson called Delaware his home for 55 years.

He returned to the game in the 1950s as a scout and spring-training coach. Stories say that he could have signed Hank Aaron for the Philadelphia Athletics, but the team didn't want to pay Aaron his $3,500 ask. Johnson was elected to the Baseball Hall of Fame in 1975 and passed away in 1989.

Six years later, Johnson's skill and legacy would be honored by his hometown when minor-league baseball came back to

JUDY JOHNSON HOME

WHAT: A historic marker at the site of Judy Johnson's Wilmington home

WHERE: 3701 Kiamensi Rd., Wilmington, DE

COST: n/a

PRO TIP: Also stop by Frawley Stadium, 801 Shipyard Dr., Wilmington, to see Johnson's statue.

The Wilmington Blue Rocks, Delaware's minor-league baseball team, holds an annual Judy Johnson Day to honor the First State's famous player. This statue stands outside their stadium, and the Blue Rocks play on Judy Johnson Field. Photo by Rachel Kipp

Delaware and named the field in his honor. A statue of Johnson stands outside the stadium where the Wilmington Blue Rocks now play.

Later in life, Johnson reflected on the impact that segregation had on his baseball career. "I was just thrilled I lived to see the day," he said of Jackie Robinson's integration of the sport in 1947. "I was born too soon. . . . My only regret is that I didn't get the chance to make that big money."

Judy Johnson was nicknamed after Madison Stars player Judy Gans. Johnson said later: "Someone said, 'You look enough like Judy Gans to be his son.' So they called me Judy and the name stayed with me."

THE FIRST FLAG UNFURLED?

Where, according to local lore, was the United States flag flown for the first time?

Delaware was home to only one battle during the American Revolution—the Battle of Cooch's Bridge, located near modern-day Newark.

For generations, local legend said that Cooch's Bridge marked the first time that an American flag was flown in battle. Today, historians label that claim questionable, but it remains a fascinating sideline of First State history.

The battle took place on September 3, 1777, near the beginning of a British push from Elkton, Maryland, to Philadelphia, eventually taking the city and kicking the Continental Congress out.

The seven-hour fight between 1,700 British and Hessian troops and 800 American light infantrymen was "bloody" and "severe," according to accounts at the time. Twenty-four rebels and four British men were killed, with about 40 injured on each side.

As the story goes, the American troops hoisted the new nation's flag—reportedly designed by Betsy Ross—for the first time in that battle. The flag had been authorized by Congress in June. The story was supported by a monument dedicated in 1901 at the battlefield site.

Soldiers who fell in the battle were buried on the land, but historians today aren't certain where. "It's hallowed ground," says retired judge Richard Cooch.

Left: *Cooch's Bridge is seen in 1925. Photo courtesy of the Delaware Public Archives*

Right: *A copy of the Betsy Ross flag flies at a monument at the battlefield site today. Photo by Dan Shortridge*

FIRST FLAG UNFURLED

WHAT: Cooch's Bridge monument

WHERE: Dayetts Mill Road, Newark, DE

COST: n/a

PRO TIP: The Cooch's Bridge historic site, located nearby, is currently closed to the public, but the Friends of Cooch's Bridge group offers scheduled tours: friendsofcoochsbridge.org/tours/. Check out the nearby Pencader History Museum down the road to learn more about area history.

But by the 1930s, the evidence had become questioned, and the language on the monument was changed. Still, wrote Lt. Gov. Edward W. Cooch Sr. in his 1940 book on the battle, "circumstantial evidence" supported the claim: "Although this has never definitely been proved, it has likewise never been disproved."

Today, experts suggest that the odds were not in Cooch's Bridge's favor. An American infantry unit would have been built for stealthiness and did not want to have its presence known, and the American flag began as a naval banner, historians say.

In the 1980s, famed muralist Jack Lewis was commissioned to create 10 paintings depicting Delaware's bicentennial. One was of the Battle of Cooch's Bridge—only his first version did not include the flag. It took some persuasion by Cooch family members, but the flag was added. The painting hangs in Legislative Hall today.

INVENTION DOCUMENTATION

Where can you see the oddities that were used to give out patents in the 1800s?

In the early days of the American patent system, aspiring entrepreneurs couldn't just envision their innovations—they also had to build them.

From the signing of the first patent legislation by President George Washington in 1790 until 1880, the US Patent Office required inventors to create a scale model of their ideas to accompany the written description and drawings. The United States was the only country in the world with a patent system that required physical models.

One of those early patents went to E. I. du Pont, the first of nearly 50,000 that would ultimately be awarded to the DuPont company, the Wilmington-based chemical giant that began as a gunpowder mill along the banks of the Brandywine Creek.

The former mill site eventually became the Hagley Museum & Library, which includes the restored mill site and workers' homes, the original du Pont family home, and a library that is devoted to the history of business and technology in America.

Hagley began searching for E. I. du Pont's old patent models in the 1950s (none from the 19th century have ever been

---

Hagley's research collection also includes the records and histories of companies including Avon, Bethlehem Steel, and the Reading Railroad. It also has the papers of industrial designers including Marc Harrison, Richard Hollerith, Irv Koons, and Thomas Lamb.

About 100 models of the nearly 5,000-invention collection are on display at the Hagley library. Photo by Rachel Kipp

HAGLEY PATENT DISPLAY

WHAT: An exhibition of scale models of 18th- and 19th-century inventions

WHERE: 298 Buck Rd., Wilmington, DE

COST: Visiting the library is free but there is an admission cost to see the rest of the museum and grounds.

PRO TIP: Check the museum website, hagley.org, for admission information and directions for entrance and parking before you go. The facility suffered substantial damage during a storm in the summer of 2020 and some areas and entrances have been closed as a result. While repairs take place, Hagley is offering a reduced admission price and access to the library without a reservation.

located). In the early 1960s, the museum bought its first collection of other inventors' models from a New York insurance executive. The collection ballooned to nearly 5,000 models in 2016 when the museum acquired a large number of models from Alan and Ann Rothschild.

Today the collection includes tiny beds, shoes, folding chairs, and other everyday household items the inventors were trying to improve, along with more esoteric offerings, including an "improved boat for duck shooting" adorned with a swan model at each corner. There is also a mechanical dog intended to shoo away pigeons and a paper bag-folding machine.

About 100 of the models are on display in Hagley's library, and others have become parts of exhibits that the museum has organized over the years.

NYLON CAPITAL

How did a lab experiment lead to an economic boom for a tiny town?

Today, we take nylon for granted. It's in our clothes, backpacks, and toothbrushes.

But a century ago, nylon didn't exist—until DuPont Co. scientists Wallace Carothers and Julian Hill created it. Experimenting with polymers to create synthetic fibers, they succeeded in 1935 with "fiber 66." It took three more years, $27 million, and more than 230 people to figure out the secret and create a production system.

The company kept the news largely under wraps until it announced its new production plant in tiny Seaford, Delaware, in October 1938. At full operation it was projected to employ more than 1,000; that would grow to 4,600 at its height in the 1980s—and with it, the title of "Nylon Capital of the World."

"It is the biggest thing that ever happened here," said Seaford businessman Roland C. Wright.

Women's stockings were the first product, with a limited amount selling out in Wilmington in just three hours. On the first day of sales in 1940, 800,000 pairs of stockings were sold. Later in the year, with 4 million pairs produced, DuPont put them on the market—and they sold out in four days.

Nylon became essential during World War II as a key ingredient in parachutes, ropes, mosquito netting, and flak jackets. DuPont's early-1940s wartime job ads boasted of

NYLON CAPITAL

WHAT: The former DuPont nylon plant, now operated by Invista

WHERE: A historic marker is at Woodland and DuPont Roads, Seaford, DE

COST: n/a

PRO TIP: The site is private property, but the Seaford Museum, at 203 High St., has an exhibit on nylon and Seaford (see www.seafordhistoricalsociety.com/visit/seaford-museum/ for hours of operation).

Left: *Seafordians turned out in force to celebrate the announcement that DuPont would be coming to town in October 1938. Photo courtesy of the Delaware Public Archives*

Right: *Today, the largely empty Nylon Capital Shopping Center—a once-bustling retail hub—is one of the few signs left that recall nylon's impact on the town of Seaford. Photo by Dan Shortridge*

"Excellent Opportunities for Women" in Seaford: "Clean plant, excellent working conditions, modern cafeteria equipped with music . . . good wages, time and one-half pay for hours worked over forty."

It's not hyperbole to say the plant transformed Sussex County. Young people could get jobs at DuPont out of high school, spend their careers there, and retire with a sound pension.

Like much of American manufacturing, nylon production declined in Seaford over several decades. The plant eventually turned to other fibers and was sold in 2004 to Koch Industries. In 2008, owner Invista laid off 400 workers, dealing a harsh blow to the local economy. Just 100 workers were still employed at a plant that once boasted a workforce larger than the population of many Delaware towns.

Seaford's primary industries in the 1930s were producing baskets and crates, canneries, flour mills, and phosphate plants, so modern textile manufacturing was a game-changer.

COUNTING THE VOTES

In which part of Delaware does a genteel 1800s election tradition continue?

Politics is a bare-knuckled rough-and-tumble sport, especially in recent years. But in Delaware, a genteel tradition dating to the early 1800s helps calm passions after Election Day.

Sussex County is home to a completely unique event every two years known as Return Day—not Returns Day, as some say—at which winners and losers gather for a ceremonial burying of the hatchet and a carriage ride and parade around the historic Circle at the center of the county seat, Georgetown.

"Return Day is one of the important reasons why Delaware works," says Tom Carper. He should know: as a US senator and former governor, congressman, and state treasurer, he's ridden in the carriages many times.

The event has its origins in the days when election returns would take a few days to collect and count. Voters and

RETURN DAY

WHAT: An only-in-Delaware event taking place the Thursday after Election Day

WHERE: All around Georgetown, the Sussex County seat

COST: Free

PRO TIP: Enjoy the ox roast, and look out for political memorabilia announcing the next campaign.

The election returns read represent only votes cast in Sussex County, so they're sometimes lopsided. In 2008, the town crier announced that Senator John McCain had received the most votes for the White House over the Obama-Biden ticket.

A detail from a Return Day mural by famed Delaware artist Jack Lewis and 11 incarcerated men participating in a prison arts program, which hangs in a building at Delaware Technical Community College in Georgetown. Photo by Dan Shortridge

candidates would return to the county seat to hear the results read by a town crier. (With horses riding in from all corners of the county, Return Day was, a journalist once joked in a play on the famed Gallup Poll, "the first Gallop Poll.")

Today, the tradition continues. "It is the Day of Reconciliation," newspaper columnist Bill Frank once wrote. "The world would be a better place in which to live if all the nations had their respective Return Days."

RODNEY'S RIDE AND FALL

Who was that masked man? And why was his statue removed?

Schoolchildren across the country learn about Paul Revere's famous ride to warn the colonists of imminent British action. Not as famous, was the midnight ride of one Caesar Rodney, then a delegate to the Continental Congress.

In July 1776, Rodney rode pell-mell from Dover to the capital in Philadelphia to cast a vote for the Declaration of Independence—the deciding vote for the future First State, as the other two delegates were divided.

He was regarded for years as Delaware's preeminent Revolutionary-era hero, with a school district, a city square, and many other institutions named in his honor.

Rodney held numerous public offices—high sheriff, register of wills, recorder of deeds, clerk of the Orphans Court, clerk of the peace, justice of the peace, member of the General Assembly, and justice of the Supreme Court. He was also a general in the Delaware militia, represented the colony in the Stamp Congress and the Continental Congress—and was president of the state for three years.

But missing from all the recognition is a simple thing: his face. Rodney suffered from facial cancer, which brought with it a

---

Delaware's legislators voted for independence on June 15, 1776, but allowed its three congressional delegates to cast their votes as they wished. Caesar Rodney was named the acting "governor" of the new state. Today, June 15 is celebrated as Separation Day in Delaware.

The Rodney family plantation known as Byfield was located south of Dover. About 200 people were enslaved there during Caesar Rodney's lifetime. Photo by Dan Shortridge

RODNEY'S RIDE AND FALL

WHAT: The site of the former Rodney plantation, known as Byfield, where Caesar Rodney started on his ride to Philadelphia

WHERE: South of Dover, at the intersection of Rt. 9 (Bayside Drive) and Bergold Lane

COST: n/a

PRO TIP: The historic marker is located in the middle of a fork in the road with no shoulders nearby, and there is little space to safely pull over to take a look.

severe facial deformity. "His face is not bigger than a large apple," John Adams wrote in his diary. There exists no portrait painted during his lifetime, and he was said to wear a green scarf to cover his face.

In recent years, Rodney's public light has dimmed. He owned enslaved people—about 200 in total on his family's plantation at Byfield in Kent County. A famous statue of Rodney on horseback, was removed from Wilmington's Rodney Square in 2020.

In 1776, a few months before that Declaration vote, Rodney wrote to his brother about his inner feelings about the Black people whose lives he controlled: "They have done me so much damage and behaved so wickedly that I have lost all confidence in and almost all affection and feeling for them."

The historical record does not reflect what the enslaved Blacks thought of Rodney.

Upon Rodney's death in 1784, the deciding vote for American independence finally released these Blacks from bondage—but with the proviso that their freedom came only after they had continued to work for a while longer.

FROM SEA BATTLES TO SEAFOOD RESTAURANT

How did a part from a WWII aircraft carrier end up outside a Kent County restaurant?

Drive south from Dover to the beaches along Route 1, and you'll see cornfields, soybean fields, irrigation equipment, and a giant golden cast-iron propeller from an aircraft carrier.

See what, now?

Yes. It's one of the massive "screws" from the USS *Shangri-La*, to be precise.

The ship was decommissioned for good in 1971. Today the propeller sits as an instantly recognizable and attention-getting landmark outside of a Kent County seafood restaurant.

Meding & Son Seafood, near Frederica, acquired the propeller in 1990—for the sole purpose of drawing eyeballs and stomachs to the family-owned eatery, recalled owner Henry Meding. "It's a draw, and it's put us on the map," Robbie Meding told a reporter.

How much does a giant aircraft-carrier propeller cost? The current owners don't say, but Robbie laughed: "It cost more to move it than it did to buy it."

They've sandblasted it and repainted it a few times, each time in gold leaf.

The *Shangri-La* was launched in February 1944 and sailed in World War II's Pacific Theater with combat raids against Japan.

The *Shangri-La*'s propeller weighs 47,000 pounds and stands 20 feet tall. The Medings had to get it hauled from a Navy salvage yard in Bayonne, NJ.

Once aboard the aircraft carrier Shangri-La, *this propeller now catches drivers' attention along busy Delaware Route 1 near Frederica. Photo by Rachel Kipp*

Her planes also air-dropped supplies to prisoners of war. After being decommissioned from 1947 to 1951, she re-entered the fleet for cruises in the Mediterranean, Caribbean, and Atlantic, returning to the Pacific for Vietnam-era service in 1970. The ship was sold for scrap in 1988. She earned two battle stars for WWII and three for Vietnam.

GIANT PROPELLER

WHAT: A 20-foot-tall propeller from the USS *Shangri-La*

WHERE: Outside Meding & Son Seafood, 3697 Bay Rd., Milford, DE

COST: Free

PRO TIP: While you're there, stop in at the restaurant for some of its delicious Maryland crab soup or clam chowder.

YOU WANNA LIVE FOREVER?

Where can you find the secret to eternal life?

Tales of a magical spring that restores the youth of anyone who takes a sip have been around for centuries. There's a historical park in St. Augustine, Florida, where explorer Ponce de Leon supposedly landed while searching for the Fountain of Youth.

As far as anyone knows, de Leon never landed in the First State, but the city of Lewes has its own Fountain of Youth. Local lore says this dates from 1631, when the first Dutch colonists settled in the area, but newspaper reports say the spring-fed well was likely used as a water supply by Native Americans for long before that. The fountain is on property once owned by the Maull family and now owned by the local Daughters of the American Revolution chapter.

The white gazebo that marks the spot was built in 1937 by the Lewes Chamber of Commerce. The fountain was dedicated at a celebration that included 14 of the town's oldest residents holding signs that read "Long Life and Pep" and a local minister dressed as Father Time.

But soon after, the Fountain of Youth fell into disrepair. It was restored again in 1951, with the hopes of attracting tourists. At one point, a spiral conch shell cup hung from the gazebo and it was rumored to augment the regenerative

---

The fountain sits on the site of the Maull House, which was built around 1739 by local carpenter Samuel Paynter. The house was sold in 1741 to river pilot Luke Shields, who later married the widow of John Maull, another pilot, who lived next door.

FOUNTAIN OF YOUTH

The spring at the Fountain of Youth dates back hundreds of years. Photo by Dan Shortridge

powers of the spring. The cup has since gone missing, but the spring still produces water.

In 2019, a member of the DAR chapter, Patti Haas, and her husband, Ted, once again restored the Fountain of Youth, including removing two feet of muck that was keeping the well from filling and dumping 15 buckets of dirty water. They told a local newspaper that the well was once again full within an hour.

FOUNTAIN OF YOUTH

WHAT: A small gazebo marked "Fountain of Youth," over a spring reportedly discovered by the original Dutch settlers in Lewes in the 1630s

WHERE: On the canal side of the historic Maull House property, 536 Pilottown Road, Lewes, DE

COST: Free

PRO TIP: Further down Pilottown Road is another well marked with a white gazebo. "Black Harry's Spring" was restored in the 1940s by the Works Progress Administration. Fed by the same spring as the Fountain of Youth, it's named for a coach driver who traveled America as a preacher spreading the word of Methodism.

TINY BIRDS

Why does part of a state park shut down each year?

Each spring and summer at one of Delaware's most popular parks, an area jutting out like a thumb into the Delaware Bay is shut to visitors.

The closure of the "Point" and other areas at Cape Henlopen State Park is part of a three-decade-long effort to protect the piping plover, a diminutive shorebird considered endangered in the First State and threatened according to the federal government.

In 1980, there were 32 adult plovers recorded in the state; eight years later, there were just seven. Special state protections began in 1990. Things are looking up: In 2021, there were a record high number of nesting plovers, with 24 pairs and 19 fledglings.

Plovers tend to lay their nests right on the beach, so restricting humans from disturbing their habitat by walking or driving on the coast is a must. In recent years, they've also nested in Prime Hook National Wildlife Refuge.

When we say they're tiny, we mean it: Baby plovers are "about the size of a piece of popcorn," the late environmental reporter Molly Murray once wrote in a memorable turn of phrase. Adults are about as big as a just-hatched chicken.

TINY BIRDS

WHAT: Nesting areas for the piping plover

WHERE: Cape Henlopen State Park

COST: n/a

PRO TIP: Rather than trying to catch a glimpse of the birds while certain areas are closed, volunteer to help monitor the nesting areas and educate the public. Call the state environmental agency at 302-735-3612.

Right: *Delaware's plover population is recovering, thanks to protective measures like closing down part of a state park. Photos courtesy of the US Fish & Wildlife Service*

Left: *A piping plover minds its eggs.*

Humans aren't the only threats to the plovers. Dogs, foxes, feral cats, crows, and grackles prey on the little fowl. If state officials spot a nest, they build an enclosure to protect it.

Plovers breed for three or four months a year, usually arriving in Delaware in March. The babies can fly about 30 days after they hatch, and the plovers begin heading south in September.

Piping plovers were a common sight along the coast in the 1800s, but almost died out when they were hunted for their feathers for use in hats.

CORPORATE CAPITAL

Why is Delaware home to so many Fortune 500 companies?

Business is big business for Delaware.

More than 60 percent of all Fortune 500 companies are formed in the First State. Ditto for a majority of New York Stock Exchange-listed companies. And more than 75 percent of all new IPOs are from Delaware-based firms.

These companies don't have physical offices, headquarters, sales floors, or manufacturing operations here. But Delaware is their state of incorporation, thanks in large part to a business-friendly legal tradition dating back to 1792.

To form a corporation here can take less than an hour; the state corporations office allows documents to be uploaded until midnight most weeknights. The state and private vendors have streamlined the process to make it as easy as possible for entrepreneurs and others to create their businesses here.

At 1209 North Orange Street in Wilmington sits a long brown-brick building with a green awning over the front door. The offices of the Corporation Trust Company, one of many such vendors and service providers known as "registered agents," are the legal home of more than 285,000 businesses, including Google, Ford, Apple, and Berkshire Hathaway.

The situation has sometimes led to a sharp eye from investigators and prosecutors, who say the anonymity and ease

CORPORATE CAPITAL

WHAT: Headquarters of the Corporation Trust Company

WHERE: 1209 N. Orange St., Wilmington, DE

COST: Free

PRO TIP: Learn more about Delaware's easy incorporation process from the state Division of Corporations: de.gov/topics/incorporateindelaware.

Behind the doors at the Corporation Trust Company offices in Wilmington is the legal location of companies such as Apple and Google. Photo by Dan Shortridge

of incorporation make Delaware's laws rife for abuse by money launderers and drug traffickers, among other criminal types.

Some states have tried to go after Delaware's golden goose, which generates millions for state coffers, by setting up their own similar court systems. But, notes Temple University emeritus law professor and former Delaware US Senate candidate Jan Ting, "They won't have the large body of Delaware case law, court rulings, generated over many years that provide both guidance and predictability."

Delaware isn't entirely the Wild West of corporations. In 2020, a judge dissolved six companies that were used by former Trump campaign officials to launder $75 million from Ukraine.

FROM KAHUNA TO KIDS

Which local museum used to be a popular city watering hole?

When you visit the Delaware Children's Museum, you're following in the footsteps of John Mayer, Green Day, Bob Dylan, and Hall & Oates.

While those musical acts have never frolicked on the DCM's 30-foot climbing structure or splashed in its water table (at least, not as far as we know) they all played in the big yellow building on the Wilmington Riverfront in its former life as the Kahunaville nightclub.

A 7,000-person venue known for the giant volcano at one outside corner, Kahunaville was the center of Wilmington's nightlife scene from 1995 until its abrupt closure in 2006. Venue lore says it was once the kind of place where women took their tops off and comedian Artie Lange once kicked a poinsettia plant into a fan's face.

Three years—and one $11 million renovation—later, the building came back to life as a museum that focuses on

THE BIG KID-HUNA

WHAT: Delaware Children's Museum, the former site of the Kahunaville nightclub

WHERE: 550 Justison St., Wilmington, DE

COST: $12 for those 1 and over

PRO TIP: The DCM offers extended hours with reduced admission from 5 to 8 p.m. on Fridays.

In 2015, Riverwalk Minigolf, an 18-hole miniature golf course, opened on the site of Kahunaville's former summer stage and tiki bar.

Once a popular nightclub, this building now houses the distinctive bright yellow Delaware Children's Museum at the Wilmington Riverfront. Photo by Rachel Kipp

educational fun for kids 12 and under. Visitors can climb through a preserved, hollowed-out 350-year old sycamore tree from Wilmington's Alapocas Woods, learn how the human body works, and manage a till of play money at a pretend cafe. There's a dedicated space for the smallest learners, including a toddler-sized train and auto shop.

The fun going on in the building may be more G-rated these days, but there's still plenty of it.

LAID TO REST

Why are British Royal Navy sailors who died in 1798 buried in a small Delaware town?

On a stormy May night in 1798, a British ship foundered off Delaware's Atlantic coast, and 32 sailors were lost to the sea.

It wasn't until 1984 that their remains were located by a team of treasure hunters, 80 feet beneath the waters of the Delaware Bay.

The sailors' bones were eventually recovered—accidentally—along with artifacts from the ship, the HMS *DeBraak*. Once they were brought ashore, the decision was made to honor the sailors with a land burial.

In 1998, exactly 200 years to the day after the shipwreck, their remains were interred underneath a gravestone outside Lewes's Zwaanendael Museum, which traces the history and maritime heritage of the area.

More than 1,000 people attended the services for the British sailors, which involved a four-block funeral procession with pallbearers, a British funeral march, and a consecration of the burial site by a Royal Navy chaplain.

A headstone at the museum site lists all the sailors who perished.

"People in Lewes offered hospitality and kindness to the sailors," recalled Chaplain Bernard Clarke. "That's why it's

---

The *DeBraak*'s captain, James Drew, is buried in St. Peter's Episcopal Church cemetery. Drew's body was the only one known to have been found after the wreck.

The remains of 32 sailors are interred, and their names memorialized, on a museum's grounds in downtown Lewes. Photo by Dan Shortridge

appropriate that those who did not survive have their final resting place here in Delaware."

Part of the *DeBraak*'s hull is on display in a special preservation building in Lewes, with occasional tours to see the remnants of the ship.

DEBRAAK CREW GRAVE

WHAT: The grave of 32 sailors of the HMS *DeBraak*

WHERE: On the grounds of the Zwaanendael Museum, 102 Kings Hwy., Lewes, DE

COST: Free

PRO TIP: To learn more about the *DeBraak* and local history, visit history.delaware.gov/zwaanendael-museum/ for museum hours and tours.

BEVERAGE BONANZA

Where can you buy beer based on ancient recipes?

You know that wine gets better with age, but how about beer?

Milton's Dogfish Head Brewery has been testing the theory since the 1990s, crafting beers made from or inspired by ancient recipes.

A partnership with University of Pennsylvania molecular archeologist Patrick McGovern, an expert in ancient beverages, produced a series of "Ancient Ales." The first one was Midas Touch, which was made with ingredients found in 2,700-year-old drinking vessels from the tomb of King Midas. It's a sweet yet dry beverage that tastes like a combo of beer, wine, and mead.

The partnership with McGovern also produced Chateau Jiahu, with an ingredient list that came from a 9,000-year-old tomb in China that marked the discovery of the oldest known fermented beverage in the history of civilization.

Dogfish Head has also experimented with other "liquid time capsules," as the brewery calls them on its website. Sah'tea is a spin on a Finnish beer from the 9th century. The beer is caramelized over white-hot river rocks, fermented with a German weizen yeast, and flavored with black tea and juniper berries gathered in the Finnish countryside.

More recently, the brewery came up with You Don't Count Carbs on a Cold, Cold Night after reading a story about ancient

HISTORY-MAKING BEER

WHAT: Beer made from or inspired by ancient recipes

WHERE: Dogfish Head Brewery/ Tasting Room, 6 Cannery Village Center, Milton, and brewpub, 320 Rehoboth Ave., Rehoboth Beach.

COST: Varies

PRO TIP: The tasting room and brewpub menus vary and Dogfish Head is always trying out new brews, so be sure to check online to see what's on tap: www.dogfish.com/ restaurants/brewpub/on-tap.

The ancient alcohol recipes are just another reason to visit the Dogfish Head brewpub in Rehoboth Beach. Photo by Rachel Kipp

potato beer. Using locally grown organic sweet potatoes, the beer is a savory brown ale with notes of warming ginger, sage, and vanilla.

The brewer's Milton tasting room and Rehoboth Beach brewpub are the best places to sample some of Dogfish Head's ancient recipes—they will often get exclusives, or have rarer recipes on tap long after they're not available widely in stores. And in the case of the Milton location, you can also book a time to take the brewery tour before tasting and see how Dogfish Head crafts its quirky concoctions.

You can still find Midas Touch, Dogfish Head's first Ancient Ale, at the café at the University of Pennsylvania's Museum of Archaeology and Anthropology in Philadelphia.

TRIBAL TOTEM

How did this wooden sculpture and landmark become the third of its kind, and why did it almost end up somewhere else?

Visitors to Delaware's beach communities might be confused to get directions to Bethany Beach that include "turn left at Chief Little Owl." But for the past 46 years, the 24-foot sculpture has come to symbolize one of the state's so-called "Quiet Resorts."

The current sculpture, which is carved from red cedar from Alaska, is actually the third of its kind to grace the prominent spot at the entrance to downtown Bethany Beach. The first one was carved by artist Peter Wolf Toth and gifted to the city in 1976. The sculpture depicts a real leader of the Nanticokes—Charles C. Clark, a World War I veteran who served as chief from 1933 to 1971—and is part of a series by Toth paying tribute to Native American tribes in all 50 states and the Canadian provinces and territories.

The first Chief Little Owl was damaged in a storm in 1992, and when city leaders tried to fix it, they discovered the statue had been invaded by termites and rot. The second version was actually sculpted by another artist, Dennis Beach. But in 2000 that sculpture also had to be taken down due to rot.

CHIEF LITTLE OWL SCULPTURE

WHAT: A 24-foot totem pole at the entrance to downtown Bethany Beach

WHERE: In the median strip of Garfield Parkway at the Rt. 1 intersection, Bethany Beach, DE

COST: Free

PRO TIP: While you can see the sculpture easily from the road for free, you'll have to park to take a close look, which costs money during the summer months.

The sculpture's face is that of Nanticoke Chief Charles C. Clark, who led the tribe for nearly 40 years. Photo by Rachel Kipp

Toth created the sculpture visitors see today. When the sculpture was put in place in 2002, it was blessed by a descendant of Little Owl. It was created from wood that is supposed to last for 50–150 years, guaranteeing that Little Owl will keep watch over Bethany for decades to come.

Peter Wolf Toth's Maryland sculpture, a 20-foot statue carved out of 100-year-old white oak, pays tribute to the Assateague tribe and can be found just to the south of Bethany Beach at Inlet Park in Ocean City, MD.

RIGHT UP YOUR ALLEY

Where can you see Delaware's most historic alley?

Founded in 1640, much of the Old New Castle historic district looks much the same as it did during the Revolutionary War period when it was Delaware's capital city. Tucked between houses on the Strand and leading to the Delaware River, the block-long Packet Alley looks fairly unassuming.

But a historic marker posted on the street lets passersby in on its notable place in history: up until the mid-1800s, New Castle was a major transportation hub for people and goods traveling up and down the East Coast. During that time, Packet Alley was where packet boats from Philadelphia met stagecoaches that were headed for Frenchtown, Maryland. From there, they would catch boats to Baltimore and another stagecoach to Washington, DC, saving about 400 miles of having to sail around the Delmarva Peninsula.

That means when you walk into Packet Alley, you're literally following in the footsteps of some famous historical figures, including seventh President of the United States Andrew Jackson, Congressmen and Secretaries of State Henry Clay and Daniel Webster, plus Confederate General Stonewall Jackson, US Senator and Republic of Texas President Sam Houston, and frontier hero Davy Crockett.

New Castle's importance in regional trade declined once rail lines were constructed between Philadelphia and Baltimore,

Packet Alley was also the subject of an eponymous 1951 children's book about twins Cathie and Ted, who meet a mysterious stranger who loans them magic glasses that allow the children to see into the past.

Packet Alley's "packet boat" connection to horse-drawn coaches gave long-distance travelers a shortcut, 1800s style. Photo by Rachel Kipp

bypassing New Castle with a stop in Wilmington. But the city's decline in national importance is one of the reasons the alley, along with many of the city's Colonial- and Federal-style houses, survived to the present day, allowing visitors to get an authentic peek into the past.

WALK IN THE FOOTSTEPS OF FAMOUS FIGURES

WHAT: Packet Alley

WHERE: Delaware River side of the Strand, midway between Harmony and Delaware Sts., New Castle, DE

COST: Free

PRO TIP: There is plenty of other history to soak up in Old New Castle, along with pretty views of the Delaware River. The Old Court House on Delaware Street is where the Declaration of Independence was read and the site of the drafting of the state's constitution. For a colonial-style meal, check out Jessop's Tavern, housed in a building that dates to 1724.

JEWISH NAME GAME

Who are all the people on the walls of a popular beach deli?

Even if you're not local, you're guaranteed to see some familiar faces inside Rosenfeld's Jewish Deli in Rehoboth Beach.

The restaurant's walls feature a continually evolving mural featuring famous Jewish people. There's everyone from US Supreme Court Justice Ruth Bader Ginsburg and Olympic swimming great Mark Spitz to Bob Dylan, the Three Stooges, and rapper Drake.

Owner Warren Rosenfeld says he knew he wanted to do a mural from the minute he signed the lease on the space about seven years ago. Thomas Scott Roberts, a well-known cartoonist who lives locally, drew the initial 25 people in a style that pays homage to legendary caricaturist Al Hirschfeld (himself a famous Jewish person.) The very first caricature to go up was former *Saturday Night Live* cast member Gilda Radner.

The famous folks are grouped together, with one area devoted to comedians, one to musicians, and another to academia and sports stars. "I wanted to keep it light-hearted," Rosenfeld said. "My original idea for Albert Einstein was that he would be holding one of those bombs with a long fuse like you see on Bugs Bunny, but we changed it to a piece of cake."

Later on, a second artist, Kathy Denk, added some color to the original black-and-white caricatures and also began adding

EAT SURROUNDED BY FAMOUS FACES

WHAT: A mural of famous Jewish people at Rosenfeld's Jewish Deli

WHERE: 18949 Coastal Hwy., Rehoboth Beach, DE

COST: Seeing the mural is free, but plan to stay and eat!

PRO TIP: Stumped by some of the people depicted on the walls? Ask a staffer for one of the restaurant's "cheat sheets."

134

We're not going to give the answers away! Visit for a good nosh, and pick up a cheat sheet while you're there. Photo by Rachel Kipp

drawings to the wall. Her method of creating a stencil from a photo and then projecting the stencil on the wall to trace the final drawing allows new famous faces to be added quickly—a key concern, Rosenfeld said, because the work has to be done in the mornings before the restaurant opens.

Recent additions include musicians David Lee Roth, Joey Ramone, Pink, and actress Scarlett Johansson wearing her Black Widow costume (which went up next to the drawing of the character's creator, comic book icon Stan Lee). Rosenfeld says he plans to keep adding people to the mural until he runs out of space.

"Some people come in and ask what's the significance of the wall," Rosenfeld says. "And I say: 'Everybody's Jewish!'"

The Rosenfeld's location in Wilmington features a smaller-scale mural of famous Jewish faces, including Jack Benny and Billy Joel.

LANDING ZONE

Where did the first European colonists plant their flags in what would become Delaware?

Between the north and the south, there are competing stories told about the first European settlement in what is now Delaware. Both areas can lay claim to a historical first, depending on how you slice it.

The first settlement was a Dutch encampment along the southern coast, at Lewes, in 1631. But that colony lasted only a year, with all settlers dead after an attack by local Native Americans.

As it would happen, the first *permanent* settlement would be at the northern end of the state, near Wilmington. A two-ship Swedish expedition landed there in 1638, and 25 colonists built Fort Christina, named to honor the queen of Sweden at the time.

Sweden? Yes, Sweden. In the 1700s, the nation dominated the Baltic Sea, and had plans to reach into the colonies on the opposite side of the Atlantic. The Swedes dominated trade in the region—known as "New Sweden"—for several decades, stretching into New Jersey, Maryland, and Pennsylvania, and Fort Christina was their center of government.

But it was still a tiny colony, with few resources and little support from the Swedish crown. "I look at myself at least 100 times a day in this mirror . . . for I sit here alone and there are hardly 30 men, of all that are here upon whom I can rely," the colony's governor wrote in 1644.

One of the Swedish ships that carried colonists here was the *Kalmar Nyckel*, a reproduction of which sails today.

A large mural facing the Fort Christina site depicts the landing of the Swedish ships and early contact with the Native American tribes. Photo by Rachel Kipp

An attempt to take the Dutch Fort Casimir—now the town of New Castle—succeeded in 1654, but the next year a Dutch force retook their fort and seized Fort Christiana shortly thereafter. New Sweden came to an end. (The English would be next to control the area, taking over from the Dutch in 1664.)

Despite being relatively short-lived, New Sweden did leave both a cultural and architectural legacy. Historians say the Swedish colonists brought with them the Lutheran brand of the Christian religion as well as the log cabin.

THE LANDING OF THE SWEDES

WHAT: The historic site of Fort Christina, capital of New Sweden

WHERE: 1110 E. 7th St., Wilmington, DE

COST: Free to visit, small charge for tours.

PRO TIP: Fort Christina is only open from Memorial Day weekend through Labor Day.

ONE HUNDRED, TWO HUNDRED

What's the archaic property system only used by Delaware?

What's a hundred?

It's not the start of a joke, but a question newcomers to Delaware ask every year.

Hundreds are a legal device that describes the land underneath parcels and municipal and county boundaries, similar to townships in other states. They were once active government tools—delineating where you voted and used for tax reporting.

But unlike, say, an Ohio township, the hundred today is not a government, and has no existence outside of property records and zoning files. Delaware is the only state that still actively uses the term hundreds.

While they were originally used by William Penn for tax purposes, the exact origins are unclear. Historians know more about what they aren't than what they actually were.

They aren't areas that mustered 100 soldiers to fight in the War of Independence. They aren't 100 acres. They aren't the land occupied by 100 families. And they aren't the area covered by 100 animal pelts.

Those are all myths that have propped up the odd story of the hundreds over the years, but they're just myths.

The hundred also lives in today on the name of a prominent group in northern Delaware—the Council of Civic Organizations of Brandywine Hundred, a nonprofit umbrella organization of more than 120 groups.

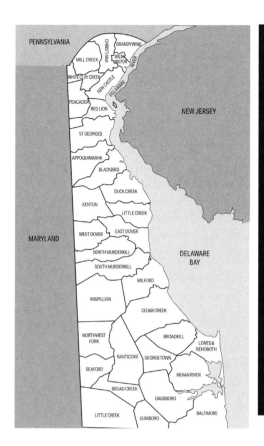

DELAWARE'S HUNDREDS

WHAT: The 33 hundreds of Delaware

WHERE: Wherever you stand, you're on a hundred, but there's an informational kiosk about their history on Dayett's Mill Road, Newark, DE.

COST: n/a

PRO TIP: If you visit a meeting of the Sussex County Council or the Planning and Zoning Commission, you'll hear each project's location identified by hundred.

Map by Hanna Manninen

We do know that the exact boundaries of the hundreds have changed over time. For example, Cedar Creek Hundred was shrunk into its current form when the county boundaries were drawn between Kent and Sussex, along the Mispillion River. Georgetown Hundred first existed from 1833 to 1835, then was reformed by the legislature in 1861. The city of Wilmington was part of Christiana Hundred until the 1830s, when it became its own.

Until the 1960s, Delaware based representation in one house of the legislature on geography, roughly following the hundreds, and in the other house on actual population. In 1964, the US Supreme Court struck the practice down in an 8–1 vote.

Today, hundreds are part of the legal description of each piece of land in the state—so tracing your home's history often requires knowing its hundred. They can also be helpful in tracking people through historic US Census records.

139

LONG-LIVED TREES

What's behind the growth of these "bald" water-loving trees?

The bald cypress is an unassuming tree, mainly found in the swamps of the South and historically chopped down for roofing shingles.

But the cypress also has some secret powers—incredibly strong and durable, it's been called "the wood eternal." The coffins of mummies and the doors of St. Peter's in Rome were reputed to have been made from its wood. They have been recorded to grow up to 1,200 years old, rising 150 feet tall.

And adding to the strangeness, Delaware marks the northernmost location of bald cypress in the United States. Trussum Pond and Trap Pond, both outside Laurel in western Sussex County, are prime bald cypress habitats. (It's called "bald" due to its largely bare branches.)

In the 1800s, a large portion of southern Sussex County and Maryland was covered by a swamp estimated to be up to 60,000 acres, today known as the Great Cypress Swamp. The trees were cut down and their wood used for shingles (cypress singles will last up to 30 years), siding, and buckets. Much of the swamp was drained for farmland, and it was wounded by several fires; one in 1930 burned for eight months.

The trees' most distinctive feature are their "knees," knobby protrusions that grow up from the roots. The exact purpose is not known, but they're believed to both feed oxygen to the roots and anchor the tree.

Left: *Canoeists and kayakers enjoy paddling around stands of cypress at Trap Pond State Park. Photos by Dan Shortridge*

Right: *Bald cypress "knees," seen in the foreground, are thought to help stabilize the trees and send oxygen into the roots. Photo by Dan Shortridge*

Today, more than 10,000 acres in the Great Cypress Swamp are owned and maintained by Delaware Wild Lands, which works to reforest the area and restore the wetlands. Part of the challenge with growing new cypress stands is that the tree is very particular in its needs, particularly with sunlight.

CYPRESS TREES

WHAT: The trees can be easily spotted in several swamps and ponds in Sussex County.

WHERE: Trap Pond State Park and Trussum Pond, outside of Laurel.

COST: Park entrance fees are in effect from May 1 to November 30 each year; see destateparks.com for current rates.

PRO TIP: For up-close views and the best photographs, bring a boat or rent one at Trap Pond during the summer season.

THE BIRDMEN OF DELAWARE

Why is the state bird a chicken?

On the surface, the blue hen chicken doesn't seem to have a lot going for it in terms of its qualifications to be Delaware's state bird. For one thing, it's not even a recognized breed of chicken. For another, it's not native to Delaware, or even the United States.

So, how did this odd bird out become so emblematic of Delaware that it's not only the state bird, but also the mascot of the University of Delaware and the namesake of any number of local small businesses and office buildings?

It all starts back in the time of the Revolutionary War, with a group of soldiers from Kent and Sussex counties led by Capt. John Caldwell. In those days, it was not uncommon for groups of soldiers to travel with chickens they would use in cockfighting tournaments during their downtime. This Delaware regiment went to battle bearing blue hens, or more accurately, blue roosters. These chickens earned a reputation for being particularly fierce and soon the entire regiment was referred to as "the Blue Hens."

The name stuck and in 1911, the University of Delaware adopted the "fightin' blue hen" as its mascot. Fast-forward another 30 years and the state was in the market for a signature bird. Some argued that the blue hen shouldn't be picked because it wasn't a wild fowl or, as a show bird with no practical

When Delaware sought to declare an official state bird in 1939, among the other contenders were a Great Blue Heron and a mourning dove.

Left: *The University of Delaware's campus, where this statue is located, has perhaps the largest concentration of blue-hen symbols in the entire state. Photo by Rachel Kipp*

Right: *The "fightin' blue hen" motif lasted into the 1800s, such as this 1864 depiction of the blue hens stamping out Copperheads, a Democratic faction that wanted to settle for peace with the Confederacy. Photo courtesy of the Delaware Public Archives*

use, particularly common. But ultimately, despite what papers at the time called "steamroller" tactics to give another bird the crown, the blue hen won the day.

The University of Delaware has a small flock of blue hens—which are more of a steel-gray than blue—on its research farm that are descendants of those bred and donated in the 1960s by S. Hallock du Pont. But researchers say those birds, a strain of the Blue Andalusian breed, aren't the same genetically as the fighting gamecocks owned by the Revolutionary War regiment. In 2016, the former state veterinarian donated three new birds to the flock.

The flock is kept for teaching and research, but some of the hens have also been taken from the farm to the nearby UD football stadium to tailgate with fans.

THE DELAWARE BLUE HEN

WHAT: A sculpture of the state bird, the blue hen, on the University of Delaware campus

WHERE: The large metal bird is located at UD's Laird campus, northwest of downtown Newark. The sculpture is under the pedestrian walkway off David Hollowell Dr.

COST: Free

PRO TIP: If you want to meet a "real live" blue hen, plan to attend a University of Delaware sporting event and grab a photo with YoUDee, the school's blue-hen mascot.

143

MEETING OF METHODISTS

How did a Delaware church become known as the "cradle of American Methodism"?

Barratt's Chapel wasn't the first place where Methodists gathered in America. But it was the place where two early American Methodist leaders met in 1784, earning it the name the "cradle of American Methodism."

After that meeting between Bishop Francis Asbury and Bishop Thomas Coke, the two men discussed plans for the church's first conference, to be held in Baltimore a month later. That event would lay the groundwork for the Methodist church in the new nation.

As Coke wrote in his journal: "After the sermon a plain, robust man came up to me in the pulpit and kissed me; I thought it can be no other than Mr. Asbury, and I was not deceived."

Today, a star on the floor of the church marks the spot where the two met.

The church is also known as the oldest American church built for Methodists, by Methodists. It was also the site of the first authorized Methodist baptism and Communion offering, at the same service where Asbury and Coke met.

CRADLE OF METHODISM

WHAT: Barratt's Chapel

WHERE: 6362 Bay Road, Frederica, DE

COST: Free

PRO TIP: Visit barrattschapel.org for the latest visitation information and hours. Also on the site is the Museum of Methodism, which includes an archive, memorabilia, and a library of 4,000 historical documents.

Barratt's Chapel, more than 240 years old, was the location of the first official Methodist baptism in America. Photo courtesy of the Delaware Public Archives

A newspaper writer opined in 1902: "To Methodists, therefore, Barratt's Chapel is what Independence Hall is to all Americans."

The church had been built just a few years before, in 1780. The land was owned by Phillip Barratt, who had recently converted to Methodism. The building's interior has been renovated several times, most recently in 1842.

In 2002, Barratt's Chapel was offered up as a new resting place for Asbury's remains after the Baltimore cemetery where he had been laid to rest had fallen on financial difficulty.

SCANNING THE STARS

How did a groundbreaking female astronomer get her start?

"Oh! Be A Fine Girl—Kiss Me!"

That mnemonic used for classifying the stars is just one small part of the legacy of Annie Jump Cannon, a groundbreaking astronomer who overcame the challenges of 1900s gender attitudes to leave her mark on the universe.

The renowned scientist is best known for her work at the Harvard Observatory—but she fell in love with the stars from the window of a home right here in Delaware.

Born during the Civil War, Cannon was raised in a home still standing in downtown Dover, on State Street. She studied astronomy and physics at Wellesley College, and further studied astronomy at Wellesley and Radcliffe College.

In 1896, she began working at the Harvard Observatory as one of a group of women classifying stars. She reportedly took just seconds to look at a star spectra and classify it. Cannon's work was contained in the Henry Draper Catalogue and the Harvard Catalogue of Variable Stars. In 1938, a few years before her death, she was appointed the William C. Bond Astronomer at Harvard.

She wrote in 1931: "Of the variables, those flickering stars of great importance in studies of the cosmos, the Harvard women observers have discovered about 5000 or two-thirds of the total number now known."

Cannon was the first woman to be awarded an honorary doctorate from Oxford and the first to be elected an officer of

---

SCANNING THE STARS

WHAT: Annie Jump Cannon House

WHERE: 34 S. State St., Dover, DE

COST: n/a

PRO TIP: Cannon is buried in Lakeside Cemetery on North State Street.

This home on State Street in Dover was where famed astronomer Annie Jump Cannon got her start. Photo by Dan Shortridge

the American Astronomical Society. Today, the Annie Jump Cannon Award recognizes a postdoctoral female researcher for her past work and future promise.

In 1918, the University of Delaware bestowed an honorary degree on Cannon. But, perhaps because she was a woman, it granted her only a bachelor's degree—and just mailed it to her rather than arranging a formal presentation in person.

Her Delaware alma mater was the Wilmington Conference Academy, from which she graduated in 1880. That later became Wesley College, a small liberal-arts school in the heart of the state capital. And in 2021, Wesley became subsumed into Delaware State University, a historically black university down the road, which now owns the Cannon family home.

Annie Jump Cannon was a political activist, fighting for women's right to vote as a suffragist and member of the National Women's Party.

FEMINIST FIGHTER

What Delaware-born activist was the first Black female newspaper editor in North America?

Born a few decades after the American Revolution and a few decades before the Civil War, Mary Ann Shadd was a true trailblazer for her time—or any time.

She grew up in Wilmington as part of Delaware's free Black community, which was about 17 percent of the state's population at that time, or 13,000 people. Born in 1823 to fiercely abolitionist parents who manned a stop on the Underground Railroad, she was the oldest of 13 siblings. She had strong opinions in a time when women, especially Black women, weren't expected to be outspoken.

At age 25, she wrote a letter to the *North Star* newspaper: "We should do more and talk less . . . . We have been assembling together and whining over our difficulties and afflictions, passing resolutions on resolutions to any extent." The editor, Frederick Douglass, ran the fiery missive. It was her first published writing—but would not be her last.

Delaware was a slave state, with about 4,500 enslaved people in 1820, and banned the education of free Black people. Shadd's family moved in 1833 from Wilmington to Pennsylvania, which was fully a free state and where their children could get an education. Shadd studied at a Quaker school and became a teacher herself.

The Shadd family has also gotten recognition in recent years with a new historical marker near Wilmington's Peter Spencer Plaza. Patriarch Abraham Shadd was an abolitionist and cobbler; he and his wife, Harriet, had 13 children.

A historical marker has also been erected near Spencer Plaza in Wilmington honoring the contributions of the Shadd family. Photo by Rachel Kipp

FEMINIST FIGHTER

WHAT: The Mary Ann Shadd Cary Post Office

WHERE: 500 Delaware Ave., Ste. 1, Wilmington, DE

COST: Free

PRO TIP: Also take a drive over to Washington, DC, where her house on W Street is a National Historic Landmark.

She taught in New Jersey, Pennsylvania, Delaware, and New York City. In 1850, after Congress passed a law to punish people who helped enslaved people escape from bondage, she and other free Blacks moved to Canada. In 1853, she founded and published the weekly *Provincial Freeman* newspaper in Chatham while continuing to teach. A few years later, she married Thomas Cary, a barber; he passed away in 1860, leaving Mary Ann Shadd Cary a single mother of two children.

Despite the challenges she faced, her remarkable list of accomplishments grew: the first Black woman to be a recruiter for the US Army. The first Black woman to earn a law degree in the United States. A suffragist who founded the Colored Women's Progressive Franchise Association in 1880. Douglass himself once wrote: "We do not know of her equal among the colored ladies of the United States."

Mary Ann Shadd Cary passed away in 1893, and is buried today at a cemetery in Landover, Maryland, about 10 miles from her former Washington, DC home.

EVERY WEEK IS SHARK WEEK

What's the "reel" story behind this fake shark?

It's Delaware's version of *Jaws*.

Motorists driving along State Route 13 have been known to stop short when they spot the giant shark mounted in a glass box outside Captain Bones Bait Tackle and Hunting near Odessa. Some use it as a gathering spot: "Meet me at the shark," they tell friends or relatives. Children sometimes write letters to it.

But how did it get there? Captain Bones was opened in 1979 by Patricia Foley and her husband, Danny. The store got its name from Danny's nickname, and it was he who decided to come up with a roadside attraction to lure in customers. At first, he parked his old crab boat out front.

Then Danny got a better idea. In 1989, his nephew, Richard H. Reed, and four fishing buddies aboard the charter boat *Shamrock* caught an 840-pound mako shark off the Delaware coast. Reed, who also managed Captain Bones at the time, told a newspaper after the catch: "Some guys fish an entire lifetime without having an experience like that."

The original shark was divided up among the fishermen and the meat eaten, though they kept some of its teeth. Danny worked with a company in Florida to make a fiberglass mount to the shark's exact measurements (his wife says that Danny, who

---

The 840-pound catch that was the inspiration for the model shark at Captain Bones set a state record for fisherman Richard H. Reed. It was beaten in 2000 by a 975-pound catch by Thomas Barnes.

The shark is modeled on a real 840-pound mako caught in 1989. Photo courtesy of Captain Bones Bait, Tackle and Hunting

DELAWARE'S 'JAWS'

WHAT: A fiberglass replica of an 840-pound mako shark caught off the coast of Delaware

WHERE: Captain Bones Bait, Tackle and Hunting, 3195 S. Dupont Hwy., Odessa, DE

COST: Free

PRO TIP: Captain Bones has no set hours, but it's open daily. A newspaper article about the real-life catch that inspired the model is posted inside the store.

died in 2001, would never tell her how much he spent on the mount). A neighbor made the wooden box.

One Christmas, the Foleys added a Santa hat to the shark's head and just never took it off. Now it's become part of the fish tale. In February 2022, the shark was damaged when a car hit its enclosure, but the owners planned to restore it to its place of honor.

"We're going to get it fixed," Patricia Foley told a local newspaper. "It means a lot to so many people."

SKATING FOR THE BLUE AND GOLD

How did this local ice rink gain a reputation for training Olympic champions?

The University of Delaware's Fred Rust Ice Arena has been a stop along the way to figure skating excellence for generations of skaters—including US Olympians such as Kimmie Meissner, Johnny Weir, and Tara Lipinski, but also athletes who have competed across the globe and at the American junior and collegiate level.

Rust Arena's reputation as a skating mecca dates back to the 1970s when the late Ron Ludington, a skating coach, moved his training base to Delaware from Detroit. He initially coached in Wilmington, but his athletes often had to get ice time late at night and early in the morning because the rink would give precedence to ice hockey.

After Ludington coached several skaters to berths at the 1984 Olympics, including pairs silver medalists Kitty and Peter Carruthers, he worked with the state and the University of Delaware to build Fred Rust Arena, and then hired a cadre of coaches to work with skaters at all stages of their careers.

In addition to being a place where skaters could receive Olympic level coaching, the University of Delaware also

---

SKATE LIKE AN OLYMPIAN

WHAT: Fred Rust Ice Arena

WHERE: 547 S. College Ave., Newark, DE

COST: Varies; public skating is $7 for adults and $5 for kids 12 and under

PRO TIP: Public skating is offered from 1 to 3 p.m. on Saturdays and Sundays

Left: *The skating center has been home to Olympians (and current Olympics skating commentators) Tara Lipinski and Johnny Weir. Photos by Rachel Kipp*

Right: *The trophy case at the arena contains awards won by skaters who trained at the center, including Olympian Kimmie Meissner.*

became a hotbed of cutting-edge skating research. For example, researchers at the university have built a computer simulation that allows skaters to see and manipulate their actual movements on a computer screen in order to improve their jumping.

But even skating novices are welcome at Rust Arena, which also offers "learn to skate" classes and open skating sessions.

The University of Delaware's figure skating team has competed in every intercollegiate National Figure Skating Championship since its inception in 2000 and has never placed below third.

CARVING ACROSS DELAWARE

What's the story behind the building of the C&D Canal?

Are you from above or below the canal?

The C&D Canal is Delaware's unofficial version of the Mason-Dixon line—on the north side are the more urban areas around Wilmington, on the south side, the gateway to the "lower, slower" lifestyle of rural New Castle and Kent County and the Sussex County beach towns.

But the canal is also a key shipping channel—it's the third busiest in the world, behind Panama and Suez.

Discussions for a canal to reduce a ship's travel time from Baltimore to Philadelphia date to the nation's early days, and included Benjamin Franklin and fourth President James Madison. Several possible routes were discussed before planners settled on a 14-mile route between Back Creek in Chesapeake City, Maryland, to the Delaware River near Delaware City. Construction began on April 15, 1824. Heavy digging machinery didn't exist in those days, and the rock and earth along the route had to be gouged out through pure manpower.

The canal took more than five years to complete. On July 4, 1829, there was a celebration to mark the canal's opening.

DELAWARE'S CROSSROADS

WHAT: The C&D Canal, which connects the Delaware River with the Chesapeake Bay

WHERE: The Michael N. Castle Trail is a walking and biking byway that runs the length of the north shore of the canal in Delaware

COST: Free

PRO TIP: After walking the trail, head just over the state line to Chesapeake City, MD, which features restaurants, shops, and the C&D Canal Museum, which delves further in the canal's history.

Left: *Sunset along the C&D Canal near St. Georges as viewed from the Michael N. Castle Trail, which runs along the canal's north shore. Photo by Rachel Kipp*

Right: *Barges carry their loads through the C&D Canal in November 1931 at St. Georges. Photo courtesy of the Delaware Public Archives*

A mule-pulled barge became the first to traverse the route. The canal was only 10 feet deep and 66 feet wide when it opened, but it's since been widened and deepened to accommodate larger boats. The C&D Canal reduced the boat trip between Baltimore and Philadelphia by 300 miles.

Chesapeake City and Delaware City came into being because of the C&D Canal. Though the deepening and eventual straightening of the canal prevented it, each town has "City" in its name because the founders thought being located along a key shipping route would lead to them growing into large metropolises.

The shores of the C&D Canal are a hotspot for fossils—among the finds that have been discovered along the canal are a pterodactyl shoulder blade and teeth from a prehistoric goblin shark.

WATERPROOF MAGIC

What's the Delaware connection to this popular waterproof fabric?

Arctic explorers, hikers, firefighters, and police officers have been able to achieve high performance with the help of clothing made from Gore-Tex, the world's first breathable, waterproof fabric.

The innovation's origins date to 1958 and to a makeshift science lab constructed in the Newark basement of Bill and Vieve Gore. The family moved to Delaware from Utah so Bill, a chemical engineer, could take a job at the DuPont Experimental Station. Bill left DuPont to start his own company, W. L. Gore & Associates, focused on different possible uses for the non-stick coating polytetrafluoroethylene (PTFE), more commonly known as Teflon. The enterprise took off when Bill's son, Bob, then a sophomore at the University of Delaware, patented an idea to use Teflon in tape form to insulate wires.

In 1969, Bill asked Bob to come up with a way to stretch Teflon like taffy in order to create a low-cost plumber's tape. Bob experienced several failures, but one night he was able to make a rod of Teflon expand to the length of his outstretched arms, without changing its diameter. Called expanded PTFE or ePTFE, and later branded as Gore-Tex, it was stronger, porous, and more versatile than its predecessor.

THE ORIGINS OF GORE-TEX

WHAT: Gore Hall, named for and constructed with a gift by the Gore family, who discovered Gore-Tex

WHERE: 114 The Green, Newark, DE

COST: Free

PRO TIP: A historical marker honoring Gore is located outside the building, which is on the portion of the Green south of East Delaware Avenue.

Gore-Tex creator Bob Gore demonstrates the "stretch" of the new material he created. Photo courtesy of W. L. Gore & Associates

In 1976, Gore received the company's first commercial order for outdoor clothing constructed from Gore-Tex fabric. Three years later, the company invented a tape named Gore-Seam to seal the seams of garments made from Gore-Tex, which further upped its waterproof capabilities. In 1981, astronauts aboard the space shuttle *Columbia* wore spacesuits made from Gore-Tex.

Gore-Tex is also used to make guitar strings and vacuum-cleaner bags. The company has also found ways to use the technology for vascular grafts used to reconnect blood vessels and medical sutures. The Gore family has also supported the engineering discoveries of the future through numerous donations to Bob's alma mater, the University of Delaware, including an $18.5 million gift used to construct Gore Hall on the campus Green.

Along with constructing a new Georgian-style façade for Du Pont Hall in 2002, the opening of Gore Hall at the University of Delaware in 1998 completed a master plan for the UD Green that was drawn up in 1917.

REGGAE MAN

How did Delaware shape Bob Marley's songwriting roots?

When people think of the place most closely associated with reggae icon Bob Marley, his homeland of Jamaica is surely what would come to mind.

But Marley also spent a pivotal time in his life living in Wilmington, which he called home on and off from 1965 to 1977. Earlier, Marley's mother, Cedella, met and married Edward Booker while visiting Delaware and the couple ultimately decided to settle in the First State. Cedella ran Roots, a reggae music store on Market Street for many years.

When Marley first moved north in 1965, he had already enjoyed success in Jamaica, but had become disillusioned with the often-unscrupulous nature of the music industry. Marley was also newly married and wanted to earn money. He moved in with Cedella and, under the name "Donald Marley" worked as a lab assistant at DuPont and at the Chrysler plant in Newark.

The time in Delaware also turned out to be an important one for Marley as an artist. He began writing classic songs including "Sun Is Shining" and "Misty Mountain" while living in Wilmington. His song "Night Shift" even references his time working at the Chrysler plant as a forklift driver.

According to his friend Godfrey "Ibis" Pitts, Marley almost went to Woodstock—as a jewelry vendor. Pitts told a local newspaper that Marley helped make the jewelry Pitts took to sell at the famous rock concert, but couldn't be convinced to tag along.

One Love Park in Wilmington was named after one of Marley's 1997 hit songs. Photo by Rachel Kipp

"When he was in Wilmington, Bob realized that music was his destiny," Kevin McDonald, Oscar-winning filmmaker and director of the documentary *Marley*, said in 2012.

Marley returned to Jamaica and used some of the money he earned in Delaware to start a record label. He would return to Wilmington periodically, to visit his mother and to live. Some of Marley's children went to elementary school in Delaware and would stay in with Cedella Booker while Marley toured.

The playground across Tatnall Street from Cedella Booker's former home was renamed "One Love Park" in Marley's honor in 2014. One of the houses in the block also has a mural of Marley.

MARLEY'S ROOTS

WHAT: One Love Park, which honors reggae icon Bob Marley and is located across the street from his mother's former Wilmington home.

WHERE: 24th and Tatnall Streets, Wilmington, DE

COST: Free

PRO TIP: Marley fans won't want to miss the annual Peoples Festival, a tribute concert that was created by Genny and Godrey "Ibis" Pitts, two of the singer's closest friends during his time in Wilmington.

THE GOOD SHIP *DELAWARE*

What is Delaware's legacy with naval ships?

It took nearly 100 years, but a ship bearing the First State's name is back patrolling the seas in the service of her country.

The new USS *Delaware*, a submarine formally known as SSN-791, was commissioned while under way—and underwater, the first ship to be so commissioned—after the pandemic canceled the formal ceremony on land. A *Virginia*-class attack sub, the nuclear-powered *Delaware* has a crew of 132 living in its 377-foot-long tube.

The last ship to bear the name *Delaware* was a battleship, serving from 1910 to 1924. It was to be the first of many battleships and America's answer to the HMS *Dreadnought*, and cost what would be more than $113 million in today's dollars. She served in World War I in the North Sea and with the Sixth Battle Squadron, was often used as a training

USS *DELAWARE*

WHAT: The bell from the battleship USS Delaware (1910–1924)

WHERE: Outside the Delaware Public Archives, 121 MLK Jr. Blvd. N, Dover, DE

COST: n/a

PRO TIP: The Archives has a rotating set of compelling exhibits on Delaware history, and is always worth a visit.

The naming of the *Delaware* began with a suggestion in a letter to the editor. Navy veteran and US Senator Tom Carper and the congressional delegation heeded the idea, and convinced the Navy to honor the First State.

Left: *The USS Delaware's 132-member crew arrives in Wilmington for a celebration of its commissioning in March 2022. Photo courtesy of U.S. Navy / Petty Officer 2nd Class Dakota David*

Right: *This bell rang on the battleship USS Delaware, the most recent ship to bear the state's name before the current submarine. Photo by Dan Shortridge*

vessel, and was decommissioned and sold for scrap in 1924. The bell from the battleship Delaware currently stands outside of the Delaware Public Archives.

"Delaware's role in the US Navy has come full circle—from a 24-gun sailing ship protecting Philadelphia from the British on the eve of our Independence, to one of the world's most impressive vessels that can operate around the globe," wrote US Senator Tom Carper.

PIONEER POLITICIAN

How did the state's first female governor ascend to the pinnacle of political power?

She was born in the middle of the Great Depression. She dropped out of high school to tend to her family's farm. She got married at age 17. She buried two husbands. She started working in politics as a clerk in the statehouse.

PIONEER POLITICIAN

WHAT: Official portrait of governor Ruth Ann Minner

WHERE: Second floor of Legislative Hall, 411 Legislative Ave., Dover, DE

COST: n/a

PRO TIP: From the visitors' galleries, you can see the chambers where Minner served— both the House and Senate—and later presided over the Senate as lieutenant governor.

And she climbed the ladder of politics, inexorably, rung after rung, to become Delaware's first female governor.

Ruth Ann Minner was a trailblazer and trendsetter in more ways than one.

With a GED and a background in farming and running a towing business, she tapped her natural political acumen to go toe-to-toe with opponents to get the job done. As governor, she banned indoor smoking in public places, improved access to college, and launched an all-day kindergarten program.

But her political career really began as a receptionist to state representative Sherman Tribbitt. When he was elected governor in 1972, she rose along with him. In 1974, she ran for office herself, winning a seat in the legislature representing her native Milford with 64 percent of the vote.

"She had become comfortable with being the only woman in the room," recalled her granddaughter, Lisa Peel, after Minner's passing in 2021.

Gov. Ruth Ann Minner's portrait, draped in mourning colors after her death, hangs at the top of the staircase in Legislative Hall, where she spent decades as a member of the House and Senate and as lieutenant governor. Photo by Dan Shortridge

She would serve four terms in the state House and three in the state Senate before running for lieutenant governor in 1992. She served eight years in that role alongside Gov. Tom Carper, and then won the top job herself in 2000, serving two terms.

In an interview around her 85th birthday, Minner recounted how she didn't let anything hold her back: "Just imagine if I had said, 'Woe is me. I'm a widow with three kids with nowhere to go, no job and no education.' I could still be back there saying, 'Woe is me.'"

When he won the presidency in 2020, Joe Biden singled her out in his remarks: "Is that Ruth Ann?" he said, spotting her in the crowd.

ONE TOWN, TWO STATES

What's the story behind the border straddling town of Delmar?

A border is just a line on a map, really. There's usually no fence or barrier, or even a marker to tell one side from the other.

That's the basic story behind the creation of the town of Delmar—"the little town too big for one state," as the slogan says.

In reality, there are two Delmars—Delmar, Maryland, and Delmar, Delaware, each sitting on the opposite side of Delaware's southern border.

Like many Delaware towns, Delmar began with the railroad. In 1859, a line was run to the southern border and beyond. Homes were built with little regard for the exact location of the state line, and so Delmar grew in both directions, north into Delaware and south into Maryland.

Delmar, Maryland, was incorporated as a town in 1888, and Delmar, Delaware, in 1899. The two communities have worked together on joint projects for decades. A combined sewer system was finished in 1927; today, the towns' water plant is in Delaware and the sewer plant in Maryland. Separate police forces united in 1954, becoming what's believed to be the only police department in the country certified to enforce the laws of two states.

WHAT: Delmar, DE, and Delmar, MD

WHERE: State St., Delmar, DE

COST: n/a

PRO TIP: If you want to buy snacks before heading south for a day in Salisbury, MD, stop on the Delaware side—no sales tax.

Left: *The railroad gave birth to Delmar, and along the rail line today still stands an old "highball" signal used to control a train's movements once a station agent deemed the track to be clear. Photos by Dan Shortridge*

Right: *Down the middle of State Street is the state line. To the left is Delmar, Delaware; to the right is Delmar, Maryland.*

Inset: *The flags of both states fly in front of the joint Town Hall, located just over the Maryland side of the line.*

Students in both towns attend elementary school in Maryland and middle and high school in Delaware. There are joint meetings between the Delaware council and the Maryland commission, which employ a single town manager.

It was school consolidation in the 1950s that drove the unification efforts, former Delmar, Maryland, Mayor Doug Niblett once recalled. "They realized they had a common bond, they had to share."

The Maryland side of town is larger than the Delaware side—3,798 people to the south versus 2,027 people to the north.

DISEASE DEFEATER

How did a Delaware social worker-activist play a key role in stamping out tuberculosis?

In the early 20th century, a diagnosis of tuberculosis was often a death sentence. A Wilmington doctor, Joseph Wales, treated poor patients with the infectious lung disease in a small shack along the Brandywine River.

But in 1907, his money ran out. He turned to his cousin, Emily P. Bissell, for help in raising the $300 the clinic needed to get through the winter. Bissell was already a well-known activist and social worker in the city—in 1883, she founded the West End Reading Room to provide social services to immigrant families. The organization also housed the state's first free kindergarten.

Bissell's idea was inspired by a magazine article about the Danish government funding tuberculosis hospitals through selling special stamps. She didn't have a government sponsor, but convinced the local Red Cross to put that group's symbol on a stamp Bissell designed herself—boughs of holly cascading over the red cross and the words "Merry Christmas."

To print the first-ever "Christmas Seals," Bissell borrowed $40 and promised the printer she would pay the rest of the bill after selling the 50,000 stamps for a penny apiece. Though the post office banned the sale of nongovernmental items at the time, the Wilmington post office agreed to let Bissell have a

---

Despite a life's work that would be considered progressive by modern standards, Emily Bissell opposed women getting the vote—in her view, it would get in the way of their commitment to philanthropy.

Left: *The former Emily Bissell Hospital closed in 2015. Photos by Rachel Kipp*

Right: *The former state-run Emily Bissell Hospital was founded in the early 1900s.*

EMILY BISSELL

WHAT: Grave of Emily Bissell, social worker and activist who invented Christmas Seals

WHERE: Wilmington and Brandywine Cemetery, 701 Delaware Ave., Wilmington, DE

COST: Free

PRO TIP: The cemetery, which is the final resting place for many local historical figures including several former governors, conducts regular tours by appointment.

stand in their lobby. Her first day of sales was December 7, 1907.

Bissell's Christmas Seals, which people affixed to their mail as decoration, raised $3,000—10 times what her cousin Dr. Wales needed to keep going. The next year, famous local illustrator Howard Pyle donated the design for the second stamp. Since then, the Christmas Seals have had a different design each year and have grown to be one of the American Lung Association's most recognized fundraisers.

The invention of Christmas Seals earned Bissell recognition including the now shuttered state tuberculosis hospital being named in her honor. Perhaps most fittingly, nearly 40 years after her death in 1948, the US Postal Service put her face on a postage stamp.

167

SMITH'S LANDING

Where did a famous English explorer land on his journey of exploration?

In 1608, an English sailor steered a small craft up the main stem of the Nanticoke River, surrounded by forests and—occasionally—the target of arrows fired by the native peoples.

At one point he turned to the east at the wide mouth of a creek and landed long enough on the western bank to place a cross made of brass to mark his presence. He and his crew then sailed on to continue their journey of mapping and first contact throughout the Chesapeake Bay region.

His name? Captain John Smith, of Jamestown fame. And the brass cross he left behind? It was at the mouth of Broad Creek in what is now Delaware.

Before arriving at Broad Creek, Smith's crew was fired upon by Native Americans on the eastern side of the Nanticoke, but made friends with those living on the western side after giving gifts.

Today, historians describe Smith as a real estate salesman. His accounts of his travels in the Chesapeake Bay region persuaded many in England to launch more journeys of exploration. He documented his contacts with the Nanticoke tribe, whose community dates back to 1400, and the beginnings of trade between the two civilizations. He wrote about the natural areas, "overgrowne with woods" and "much frequented with Wolves, Beares, Deere, and other wild beasts."

While exploring the Chesapeake Bay region, John Smith almost died after being stung in the wrist by a stingray. His men even dug a grave at his orders.

This pillar was installed to mark the area on Broad Creek where Captain John Smith's Chesapeake Bay explorations took him to. Photo by Dan Shortridge

JOHN SMITH'S EXPLORATIONS

WHAT: Monument at Phillips Landing Recreation Area

WHERE: Phillips Landing Road, Laurel, DE

COST: n/a

PRO TIP: The area is a popular fishing spot, and features a boat launch, picnic tables, and portable restrooms. Bring your own kayak for a great paddling adventure.

But it wasn't until 2005 that an intensive computer-aided mapping analysis convinced many observers that Smith had indeed ventured up into what is now Delaware. Smith's maps were highly primitive by today's standards, but he still managed to get most of it right.

"He mapped with a stunning level of accuracy," said Salisbury University professor Michael Scott. "He's out there in this little boat navigating the hazards of uncharted territory, and he was able to capture most major bends of the river and everything is pretty close to scale."

The brass cross has not been found in the last 400 years, and is consigned to history.

RESTORING ARTISTS' VISIONS

How does a team of Delaware art experts help protect and preserve beautiful and historic objects for the future?

Delaware is home to the nation's premier museum housing the decorative arts, the former du Pont family estate known as Winterthur.

But behind the scenes, it's also home to a program to train the next generation of art conservationists—scientists and historians who meticulously analyze, preserve, and restore artworks that have been damaged by the ravages of time, water, sun, or simple neglect.

A partnership between the University of Delaware and Winterthur gives students the chance of a lifetime to learn skills that can help keep art in the public eye for generations to come—and it's one of just three art conservation programs in the nation.

Undergraduate students mainly work on the UD campus in Newark with a wide range of art and artifacts at their disposal, while graduate students pursuing their masters' degrees do their work in labs, studios, and exam rooms 15 miles to the north at Winterthur. There they can tap into the museum's vast library collections and decorative art, as well as a high-tech

RESTORING ARTISTS' VISIONS

WHAT: Winterthur Museum, Garden, & Library

WHERE: 5105 Kennett Pike, Winterthur, DE

COST: Tickets vary from $8 for children 2–11 to $22 for adults. Hours and days vary.

PRO TIP: Tours of the Winterthur conservation labs are available on select dates; call 800-448-3883 or visit www.winterthur.org/visit/plan-your-visit/ for details.

Left: *Conservator Mina Porell works on a painting. Photos courtesy of Winterthur Museum*

Right: *Conservators Mina Porell and Matthew Cushman in the paintings lab.*

analytics laboratory. A doctoral degree in preservation studies is also offered.

Students' projects are varied as they are fascinating: determining what color 1920s window shutters should be painted, investigating how to protect fragile objects from unfiltered light, and treating an 18th-century copy of a famous Persian poem.

Sometimes, the work is like being a detective. Faculty member Jennifer Mass once helped discover a hidden image under an early Picasso masterpiece using a high-tech X-ray machine that examined pigments.

The team has also done public outreach, advising people with questions about family heirlooms or prized art pieces about how to fix or stabilize them. In one instance, a group of UD students had to reconstruct a Norman Rockwell painting after someone had completely painted over it to fix minor flaws. It took months for the conservators-in-training to painstakingly remove the overlaid paint and then redo the original, working from contemporary photographs.

Students in a recent course on photograph conservation helped preserve more than 60 damaged pictures from the Tuskegee University archives dating back to the 1890s.

SOURCES

The Art of Arden
On-site visit. Milford, Maureen. "A Path through a Quirky Past." *The News Journal*, Oct. 15, 2012. Parks, Jim. "As It Nears 100, Arden Has Big Plans." *The News Journal*, July 3, 1997. Prihar, Asha. "The Village of Arden Is an Idyllic, 'Single Tax' Arts Community Just South of Philly That's Lasted over 120 Years." *Billy Penn*, Feb. 3, 2022. https://billypenn.com/2022/02/03/arts-colony-arden-delaware-single-tax-movers-and-makers/

Mitchum's Marker
On-site visit. Associated Press. "Robert Mitchum's Ashes Scattered at Sea." *The Spokesman-Review*, July 10, 1997. https://www.spokesman.com/stories/1997/jul/10/robert-mitchums-ashes-scattered-at-sea/. "Dorothy Mitchum, Widow of Actor Robert Mitchum, Dies at 94." *Variety*, April 16, 2014. https://variety.com/2014/film/people-news/dorothy-mitchum-widow-of-actor-robert-mitchum-dies-at-94-1201158469/. "Dorothy Clements Spence Mitchum." *The Santa Barbara Independent*, April 17, 2014. https://www.independent.com/obits/2014/04/17/dorothy-clements-spence-mitchum/. "Dorothy Clements Spence Mitchum." findagrave.com, n.d. https://www.findagrave.com/memorial/129550262/dorothy-clements-mitchum. Estrada, Louie. "Film and TV Star Robert Mitchum Dies at Age 79." *The Washington Post*, July 2, 1997. https://www.washingtonpost.com/archive/local/1997/07/02/film-and-tv-star-robert-mitchum-dies-at-age-79/2c7c3de9-3293-4d7c-bee6-3124b3d73d4c/. McNulty, Anne. "The Two Sides of Former Trappe Resident Robert Mitchum." *What's Up Magazine*, February 21, 2019. https://whatsupmag.com/culture/the-two-sides-of-former-trappe-resident-robert-mitchum/. Mullinax, Gary. "Little Delaware: A Pit Stop on the Road to Fame." *The News Journal*, June 6, 1999. "Robert Mitchum." findagrave.com, n.d. https://www.findagrave.com/memorial/1817/robert-mitchum.

Journey to Freedom
On-site visit. "An Illegal Activity: The Underground Railroad in Delaware." Delaware Historical and Cultural Affairs, n.d. https://history.delaware.gov/2014/08/26/an-illegal-activity-the-underground-railroad-in-delaware-exhibit-extended-through-dec-7-2014/. Billington, Mike. "Delaware and the Underground Railroad." *The News Journal*, Feb. 8, 2008. "Freedom Seekers: The Odessa Story." Historic Odessa Foundation, n.d. https://www.historicodessa.org/plan-your-visit/freedom-seekers-odessa-story. Kipp, Rachel. "Underground Railroad May Be Resurrected." *The News Journal*, Feb. 24, 2007.

Space Suit-Up
Howard, Arshon. "Lewes Man Chronicles History of ILC Dover in New Book." *The Delaware State News*, Oct. 17, 2020. https://baytobaynews.com/stories/lewes-man-chronicles-history-of-

ilc-dover-in-new-book,34952. Mallonee, Laura. "Peek Inside ILC Dover, the Company That Makes NASA's Space Suits." *Wired*, Dec. 1, 2015. https://www.wired.com/2015/12/christopher-leaman-ilc-dover/. Ruth, Eric. "Space Suit Tailor." University of Delaware, July 15, 2019. https://www.udel.edu/udaily/2019/july/apollo-space-suits-dover-ilc-industries-homer-sonny-reihm/. "Spacesuits." ILC Dover, n.d. https://www.ilcdover.com/aerospace/spacesuits/.

Big Bible
"Ceremonies Attending the Inauguration of Governor-Elect John Hunn." *The Morning News*, Dec. 8, 1900. Frank, Bill. "Bibles Have Big Role at State Inaugural." *The News Journal*, Jan. 4, 1985. Frank, William P. "History Blots Tribbitt's Number." *The Morning News*, Jan. 1, 1973. Jackson, Patrick. "Minner Tradition Is Truly Blessed." *The News Journal*, Jan. 17, 2001. "Wipe the Dust off the Official State Bible." Delaware Public Archives, Jan. 10, 2013. https://archives.delaware.gov/2013/01/10/wipe-the-dust-off-the-official-state-bible/.

War and the Wall
On-site visit. "Cannonball House." Delaware Public Archives, n.d. https://archives.delaware.gov/historical-markers-map/cannonball-house/. Galloway, Gloria. "It's Full Steam Ahead at 'Cannonball House.'" *The Evening Journal* (Wilmington, DE), Nov. 13, 1964. Murray, Molly. "Cannonball House Tells the Story of Lewes." *The News Journal*, Aug. 6, 2009. "The Lewes Maritime Museum at the Cannonball House." Lewes Historical Society, n.d. https://www.historiclewes.org/visit/society-properties/cannonball-house.html.

Mother Church
Baldwin, Lewis. "Peter Spencer's Influence on Ideas and Struggles Still Can Be Felt on Wilmington and Delaware to This Day." *The News Journal*, Aug. 13, 2006. brown, robin, "Legacy of Ex-Slave, Pastor, Lives on through August Quarterly." *The News Journal*, July 10, 2007. "History." Mother Africa Union Church. https://motherafricanunion.org/history.

The Pirates of Pyle
"Museum History." Delaware Art Museum, n.d. https://delart.org/visit/museum-history/. "American Illustration." Delaware Art Museum, n.d. https://delart.org/collection/american-illustration/. Price, Betsy. "Did You Know? Howard Pyle." *The News Journal*, Oct. 5, 2011.

The Last Ships
On-site visits, Milford and Bethel. "About Victory Chimes: Specifications." *The Victory Chimes*, n.d. https://www.victorychimes.com/shipspecs. Hoey, Kim. "Milford's Art Boats Give Visitors Reason to Linger." *The News Journal*, April 23, 2015. https://www.delmarvanow.com/story/news/local/delaware/2015/04/23/milfords-art-boats-give-visitors-reason-linger/26233113/. Hutchinson, Henry H. "Collected Notes on Bethel (Formerly Lewisville), Del." *The Archeolog*, Sussex Society of Archeology and History, March 1969. https://www.delawarearchaeology.org/wp-content/uploads/2020/12/Vol.-21-No.-1.pdf.

"History Matters: Shipbuilding Industry along the Wilmington Riverfront." Delaware Public Media, July 22, 2016. https://www.delawarepublic.org/culture-lifestyle-sports/2016-07-22/history-matters-shipbuilding-industry-along-the-wilmington-riverfront. "Milford Shipyards." Milford Museum, n.d. https://www.milforddemuseum.org/exhibits/exhibit-3/. "Milton, Delaware." Advisory Council on Historic Preservation, n.d. https://www.achp.gov/preserve-america/community/milton-delaware. Smith, Jerry. "Historic Vinyard Shipyards Could One Day Be a Part of Milford's Riverwalk." *The News Journal*, Dec. 21, 2018. https://www.delawareonline.com/story/news/2018/12/21/historic-vinyard-shipyard-eyed-part-milfords-riverwalk/2262867002/.

Hot and Cold Confections
On-site visit. Bleiweis, John. "Scorpion Sting Reigns Supreme in Delaware." *Delaware Wave*, July 9, 2013. Parrish, Amanda. "What's the Scoop?" *The News Journal*, June 19, 2021. Talorico, Patricia. "Rehoboth Ice Cream Store in Ripley's Believe It or Not." *The News Journal*, Sept. 19, 2016. "Homemade Flavors." The Ice Cream Store, n.d. http://www.rehobothbeachicecream.com/flavors.html. "The Full Scoop: Top Ice Cream Spots in Delaware." VisitDelaware, n.d. https://wwwvisitdelaware.com/top-ice-cream-spots.

Beach Bug
Appleton, Andrea. "Lights Out." *Chesapeake Bay Magazine*, June 4, 2020. https://chesapeakebaymagazine.com/lights-out/. Eichmann, Mark. "Rare Delaware Bethany Beach Firefly Approaches Endangered Species List." WHYY, Dec. 24, 2019. https://whyy.org/articles/rare-delaware-bethany-beach-firefly-approaches-endangered-species-list/. Lauria, Maddy. "Firefly Unique To Del. Loses Key Habitat." *The News Journal*, June 22, 2019.

Delaware on Guard
On-site visit. Dreiblatt, Tyler. "History of Fort Miles at Cape Henlopen State Park." Delaware State Parks Adventure Blog, Sept. 17, 2020. https://destateparks.blog/2020/09/17/history-of-fort-miles-at-cape-henlopen-state-park/. Kenton, Debbie. "Fire Control Towers." Delaware Division of Historic and Cultural Affairs, n.d. https://history.delaware.gov/preservation/firetowers/.

The Watchtowers
Murray, Molly. "One Lone Guard among Tall Trees." *The News Journal*, July 20, 2013.

Secret Warriors
"Looking for What Goes Bump in the Night." *The Air Mobility Command Museum Hangar Digest*, Vol. 13, No. 3, July–Sept. 2013. https://amcmuseum.org/wp-content/uploads/2015/01/Hangar_Digest_July_2013.pdf. "Rocket Test Program, Hangar 1301." Air Mobility Command Museum, n.d. https://amcmuseum.org/history/rocket-test-program-hangar-1301/.

Revolutionary Writer
On-site visit. "Burial Ground Identified at John Dickinson Plantation." Delaware Division of Historical and Cultural Affairs, March 23, 2021. https://news.delaware.gov/2021/03/23/burial-ground-identified-at-john-dickinson-plantation/. Calvert, Jane E. "John Dickinson Biography." The John Dickinson Writings Project, n.d. https://dickinsonproject.rch.uky.edu/biography.php. "John Dickinson Plantation." Delaware Division of Historical and Cultural Affairs, n.d. https://history.delaware.gov/john-dickinson-plantation/. Shortridge, Dan. "Scholar studies forgotten man of Revolution." *The News Journal*, Dec. 13, 2010.

Imprisoned on the Island
"Find Your Adventure at Fort Delaware." Delaware State Parks, n.d. https://destateparks.com/History/FortDelaware. Holveck, Brandon. "Haunted Delaware." *The News Journal*, Oct. 31, 2019. Magaraci, Kim. "You'll Never Forget Your Visit to the Most Haunted Restaurant in Delaware." Only In Your State, Aug. 17, 2017. https://www.onlyinyourstate.com/delaware/haunted-restaurant-in-delaware-de/. Magaraci, Kim. "This Abandoned Fort In Delaware Is One of the Most Haunted Places in the World." Only In Your State, Aug. 8, 2021. https://www.onlyinyourstate.com/delaware/ghosts-fort-delaware-de/. Mathur, Shruti. "TV's 'Ghost Hunters' Investigate State Park." *The News Journal*, April 20, 2008.

Miles's Stompin' Grounds
Arneson, Jaret. "Monster Grip: No. 48 Ally Chevy Placed on Dover's Iconic Monument." *Hendrick Motorsports*, Aug. 14, 2020. http://www.hendrickmotorsports.com/news/articles/106935/monster-grip-no-48-ally-chevy-placed-on-dovers-iconic-monument. "Miles the Monster." *AtlasObscura*, June 27, 2016. https://www.atlasobscura.com/places/miles-the-monster. "Track Facts—Monster Monument." Dover International Speedway, Feb., 11, 2021. https://www.doverspeedway.com/tabs/track-facts-monster-monument/. Durr, Tim. "5 Facts You Need to Know about the Monster Mile." Fox Sports, June, 1, 2017. https://www.foxsports.com/nascar/gallery/monster-mile-5-facts-dover-international-speedway-jimmie-johnson-richard-petty-sprint-cup-092916. Kraft, R. J. "Kraft's Korner: Is Miles the Monster the Best Trophy?" NASCAR.com, May 28, 2015. https://m.nascar.com/news-media/2015/05/28/krafts-korner-is-miles-the-monster-the-best-trophy/. "Miles the Monster." RoadsideAmerica, n.d. https://www.roadsideamerica.com/story/18216.

Separate Schools
On-site visit, Iron Hill School. brown, robin. "Education for All." *The News Journal*, Feb. 29, 2012. "Iron Hill School: An African-American One-Room School." National Park Service, Aug. 3, 2021. https://www.nps.gov/articles/iron-hill-school-an-african-american-one-room-school-teaching-with-historic-places.htm. "Old School Damaged in Fire." *The News Journal*, April 12, 2007. Shortridge, Dan. "Saving a School." *The Daily Times*, July 16, 2000.

Muskrat on the Menu
On-site visit. Kester-McCabe, Dana. "Muskrat: A Marsh Delicacy." *Delmarva Almanac*. http://delmarva-almanac.com/index.php/content/article/muskrat_a_marsh_delicacy/. Magaraci, Kim. "The Only Place in Delaware That Still Serves up a Muskrat Dinner Is Southern Grille of Ellendale." Only In Your State, Dec. 17, 2019. https://www.onlyinyourstate.com/delaware/muskrat-dinner-ellendale-de/. "About the Southern Grille of Ellendale." Southern Grille, n.d. https://www.thesoutherngrilles.com/about-the-southern-grille. Talorico, Patricia, "Delaware Diner Says Goodbye, Muskrat." *The News Journal*, Sept. 16, 2014. https://www.delmarvanow.com/story/life/food/2014/09/16/goodbye-muskrat/15756055/. Talorico, Patricia. "Muskrat Seekers Are Still among Us." *The News Journal*, Jan. 13, 2015. https://www.delawareonline.com/story/life/food/2015/01/13/muskrat-seekers-still-among-us/21687575/

Cluck, Cluck, Oops
On-site visit. Mammarella, Ken. "1923 Shipping Mistake Led to Delmarva Chicken Industry." *The News Journal*, Jan. 13, 2015. https://www.delawareonline.com/story/life/2015/01/13/shipping-mistake-led-delmarva-chicken-industry/21718231/. Williams, William H. *Delmarva's Chicken Industry: 75 Years of Progress*. Georgetown, Del.: Delmarva Poultry Industry, Inc., 1998.

Delaware vs. Delaware
Associated Press. "Pierre 'Pete' du Pont IV Dies; Ran for President in 1988." Politico.com, May 9. https://www.politico.com/news/2021/05/09/pierre-pete-du-pont-iv-dies-ran-for-president-in-1988-486256. Dionne, E. J. "Du Pont Enters the G.O.P. race for President." *The New York Times*, Sept. 17, 1986. https://www.nytimes.com/1986/09/17/us/du-pont-enters-the-gop-race-for-president.html. Flegenheimer, Matt. "Biden's First Run for President Was a Calamity. Some Missteps Still Linger." *The New York Times*, June 3, 2019. https://www.nytimes.com/2019/06/03/us/politics/biden-1988-presidential-campaign.html. Gorenstein, Nathan. "For Biden, the Issue Is Children." *The Morning News* (Wilmington, DE), June 10, 1987. Margolis, Jon, and Elaine Povich. "Biden Admits Errors, Drops Out." *The Chicago Tribune*, Sept. 24, 1987. https://www.chicagotribune.com/news/ct-xpm-1987-09-24-8703120482-story.html. Williams, Marjorie. "Pete du Pont and the Search for a Spark." *The Washington Post*, Feb. 2, 1988. https://www.washingtonpost.com/archive/lifestyle/1988/02/02/pete-du-pont-and-the-search-for-a-spark/3e710728-54b5-4bd2-86df-e4fe5235c646/. United Press International. "NJ Newspaper Endorses du Pont." *The Los Angeles Times*, Dec. 2, 1987. https://www.latimes.com/archives/la-xpm-1987-12-02-mn-17284-story.html.

Death by Chocolate
On-site visit. Dowd, Katie. "Murder by Mail: The Story of San Francisco's Most Infamous Female Poisoner." sfgate.com, Oct. 10, 2016. https://www.sfgate.com/bayarea/article/San-Francisco-murder-poison-Cordelia-Botkin-9880884.php. Drouin, Brian. "100 year old Murder Case Still Haunts Dover, Delaware." WHYY, October 24, 2014. https://whyy.org/articles/100-year-old-murder-case-still-haunts-dover-delaware-video/. Smith, Jerry. "Dover's Infamous 'Chocolate Candy Murders' Brought Back to Life On Anniversary." *The News Journal*, Aug. 1, 2018. https://www.delawareonline.com/story/news/2018/08/01/dovers-chocolate-candy-murders-brought-back-life-anniversary/862842002/.

Bean Power
"Delaware Agribusiness—Farming the 21st Century Way." Delaware Prosperity Partnership, July 19, 2019. https://www.choosedelaware.com/press-releases/delaware-agribusiness-farming-the-21st-century-way/. Kee, Ed. "Tiny Lima Beans Pack Big Punch for Delaware Farmers." *The News Journal*, Aug. 30, 2014. https://www.delawareonline.com/story/money/business/2014/08/30/tiny-lima-beans-pack-big-punch-delaware-farmers/14755063/. Kee, Ed, James Glancey, and Tracy Wootten. "The Lima Bean: A Vegetable Crop for Processing." *HortTechnology*, April-June 1997. Short, Michael. "Lima Researcher Aims to Build a Better Bean." Oct. 4, 2019, *Lancaster Farming*. https://www.lancasterfarming.com/lima-researcher-aims-to-build-a-better-bean/article_bbd1e4eb-310b-5401-bd0a-40c2f213c852.html. Thomas, Adam. "Lima Bean Lines." *UDaily*, University of Delaware, March 27, 2017. https://www.udel.edu/udaily/2017/march/disease-resistant-lima-beans/.

A Family Feud?
Talorico, Patricia. "Behind the Wall." *The News Journal*, Jan. 14, 2019. "Visit Us." Nemours Estate, n.d. http://nemoursestate.org/visit.html.

Road to the White House
On-site visit. Eaves, Ali. "As Some States Close Highway Rest Stops, Others See Roadside Revenue." Stateline blog, Pew Charitable Trusts, July 28, 2010. https://www.pewtrusts.org/en/research-and-analysis/blogs/stateline/2010/07/28/as-some-states-close-highway-rest-stops-others-see-roadside-revenue. Peterson, Josephine. "I-95 Welcome Center Renamed after Bidens." *The News Journal*, Sept. 18, 2018. Weingroff, Richard. "A Moment in Time: President John F. Kennedy Cuts a Ribbon." Highway History blog, US Department of Transportation, April 10, 2019. https://www.fhwa.dot.gov/highwayhistory/moment/kennedy.cfm.

Ancient Bloodlines
"Just Flip 'Em! Program." Ecological Research & Development Group, n.d. https://www.horseshoecrab.org/act/flipem.html. Madrigal, Alexis C. "The Blood Harvest." *The Atlantic*, Feb. 26, 2014. https://www.theatlantic.com/technology/archive/2014/02/the-blood-harvest/284078/. Pavid, Katie. "Horseshoe Crab Blood: The Miracle Vaccine Ingredient That's Saved Millions of Lives." The Natural History Museum, London, Jan. 15, 2021. https://www.nhm.ac.uk/discover/horseshoe-crab-blood-miracle-vaccine-ingredient.html. "Shorebirds and

Horseshoe Crabs on the Delmarva Peninsula." Delaware Museum of Nature & Science, n.d. https://www.delmnh.org/shorebirds/.

A Round for the History Books
On-site visit. "Golden Fleece Tavern Site." *AtlasObscura*, Feb. 15, 2019. https://www.atlasobscura.com/places/golden-fleece-tavern-site. "Golden Fleece Tavern." Delaware Public Archives, n.d. https://archives.delaware.gov/historical-markers-map/golden-fleece-tavern/. Merriweather, James. "Delaware Day Marks 215th Anniversary of Statehood." *The News Journal*, Dec. 8, 2002.

The Killer's Cranium
brown, robin. "Patty Cannon's Skull Now Spends Halloweens at the Smithsonian." *The News Journal*, Oct. 29, 2013. https://www.delawareonline.com/story/life/2019/06/13/archives-patty-cannons-skull-now-spends-halloween-smithsonian/1444832001/. MacArthur, Ron. "A Sussex County Serial Killer." *The Cape Gazette*, Nov. 30, 2018. https://www.capegazette.com/article/sussex-county-serial-killer/159135. "Marker on Del.-Md. Line Dedicated to Sordid History." WBOC, May 17, 2012. https://www.wboc.com/story/18511386/marker-on-del-md-line-dedicated-to-delmarvas-sordid-past. Sharp, Andrew. "Why a Local Development Is Named for Murderer Patty Cannon." The Delaware Independent, Jan. 5, 2022. https://www.delawareindependent.com/why-is-a-local-development-named-for-patty-cannon/.

Machinery Man
"Oliver Evans: A Better Steam Engine." PBS, Who Made America, n.d. https://www.pbs.org/wgbh/theymadeamerica/whomade/evans_hi.html. Ricci, Tom. "Oliver Evans." American Society of Mechanical Engineers, April 25, 2021. https://www.asme.org/topics-resources/content/oliver-evans. "Oliver Evans." Delaware Public Archives, n.d. https://archives.delaware.gov/historical-markers-map/oliver-evans/. "Oliver Evans." National Park Service, n.d. (Updated Aug. 27, 2021.) https://www.nps.gov/people/oliver-evans.htm.

Quarantine at the Cape
On-site visit. Tyson, Rae. "For Many Immigrants, Cape Quarantine Was First Stop." *The News Journal*, Dec. 4, 2014. Wilson, John Mark. "The Delaware Breakwater Quarantine Station." Delaware State Parks Adventure Blog, April 20, 2020. https://destateparks.blog/2020/04/20/the-delaware-breakwater-quarantine-station/.

Indiana Jones's Warehouse
On-site visit. Coulter, Elizabeth. "Collection Close-up: Protest Face Mask and Shirt," Delaware Division of Historical and Cultural Affairs, Sept. 3, 2021. https://history.delaware.gov/2021/09/03/protest-face-mask-and-shirt/. "Collections Program." Delaware Division of Historical and Cultural Affairs, n.d. https://history.delaware.gov/collections/. Kipp, Rachel. "Slice-of-Life Preservers." *The News Journal*, June 21, 2009.

The World of Wayne
"Enlighten Me: State Tourism Officials Fill in Delaware's Story for Visitors." Delaware Public Media, Sept. 30, 2016. https://www.delawarepublic.org/business/2016-09-30/enlighten-me-state-tourism-officials-fill-in-delawares-story-for-visitors. Magaraci, Kim. "A Breathtaking Bridge in Delaware, The Indian River Inlet Bridge Has an Unexpected and Dark History." Onlyinyourstate.com, March 5, 2020. https://www.onlyinyourstate.com/delaware/indian-river-inlet-bridge-de/.

Honor and Respect
"About Us: Air Force Mortuary Affairs Operations." US Air Force, May 6, 2020. https://www.mortuary.af.mil/About-Us/Fact-Sheets/Display/Article/2162189/afmao-history/. "AFMAO History." US Air Force, April 23, 2020. https://www.mortuary.af.mil/About-Us/Fact-Sheets/Display/Article/2162189/afmao-history/. Hamilton, Brian. "To Honor the Fallen: Inside the Dover Port Mortuary." US Army, Nov. 14, 2017. https://www.army.mil/article/196779/to_honor_the_fallen_inside_the_dover_port_mortuary. Jones, Montrell L. "Dover Legend Remembered." US Air Force, Dover Air Force Base, Feb. 5, 2019. https://www.dover.af.mil/News/Commentaries/Article/1748668/dover-legend-remembered/. Kelly, Mike. "Behind the Scenes at Dover Air Force Base—Where the Casualties of America's Wars Come Home." NorthJersey.com, Oct. 2, 2019. https://www.northjersey.com/story/news/columnists/mike-kelly/2019/10/02/dover-air-force-base-behind-scenes-americas-military-mortuary/2222857001/. Miller, Beth. "Dover AFB Mortuary Preparing for Casualties." *The News Journal*, March 23, 2003.

Along the Border
On-site visit, Marydel. Nathan, Roger E. "East of the Mason-Dixon Line: A History of the Delaware Boundaries." Delaware Heritage Press, 2000. https://archivesfiles.delaware.gov/ebooks/East_of_the_Mason_Dixon_Line_A_History_of_the_Delaware_Boundaries.pdf. Miller, J. L. "Heading for the Border." *The News Journal*, Oct. 14, 1999. "The Mason-Dixon Line, That Land Is Your Land." Delaware Geological Survey, March 30, 2010. https://www.dgs.udel.edu/news/mason-dixon-line-land-your-land.

Desegregation Decision
"Claymont Negroes Win School Suit." *The Journal Every Evening*, April 1, 1952. "Chapter 277, Formerly Senate Bill No. 75." Delaware General Assembly, n.d. https://legis.delaware.gov/SessionLaws/Chapter?id=20603. Gimenes, Livia. "Louis Redding: the life and legacy of a trailblazing lawyer, champion against school segregation." *The Brown Daily Herald*, Feb. 25, 2021. https://www.browndailyherald.com/article/2021/02/louis-redding-the-life-and-legacy-of-a-trailblazing-lawyer-champion-against-school-segregation. "Howard High School, National Historic Landmark Nomination." US Department of the Interior, April 5, 2005. https://npgallery.nps.gov/GetAsset/f9d27c83-1521-48fe-afc0-9eef52244889. "Howard High School of Technology." New

Castle County Vocational Technical School District, Oct. 13, 2018. https://4.files.edl.io/a56b/12/21/20/154526-d9870c33-1abf-47d5-a0c8-a693aa8d0c67.pdf. "Judicial Officers." Delaware Supreme Court, n.d. https://courts.delaware.gov/supreme/justices.aspx. McAneny, D. J. "Delaware Officials Mark State's Role in *Brown v. Board Of Education* on Anniversary." WDEL.com, May 17, 2021. https://www.wdel.com/news/delaware-officials-mark-states-role-in-brown-v-board-of-education-on-anniversary/article_46c57f56-b71f-11eb-ae55-3b067032b8f1.html. "Our History: Inspiring Future Outcomes." Friends of Hockessin Colored School #107, n.d. https://hockessincoloredschool107.org/our-history.

History and Nature
On-site visit. Billington, Mike. "Freedom Manor: Preserving Underground Railroad Stop Draws Interest." *The News Journal*, March 26, 2008. Koppeser, Adam. "Trail through time: Hunn Park comes back from brownfields." *The Dover Post*, April 20, 2016. https://web.archive.org/web/20190330050449/https://www.doverpost.com/news/20160420/trail-through-time-hunn-park-comes-back-from-brownfields.

A Beach's Bounty
Personal conversation with Molly Murray. Murray, Molly. "Has Del.'s first village been dredged ashore?" *The News Journal*, Dec. 9, 2004. Reeve, Mark S. "Diving into the Past." *Delaware Today*, June 23, 2008. https://delawaretoday.com/beach-guide/diving-into-the-past/. "Roosevelt Inlet Shipwreck." Delaware Historical & Cultural Affairs, n.d. https://history.delaware.gov/archaeology/roosevelt-inlet-shipwreck/.

Poet in the Park
On-site visit. brown, robin. "For Town of Milton, Statue of Its Namesake Will Be Poetic Justice." *The News Journal*, March 11, 2008. brown, robin. "Milton Dedicates Statue of Town's Namesake—with a Prince's Blessing." *The News Journal*, Dec. 16, 2008. Dengler, Jody. "Tourist at Home: Milton." *The Cape Gazette*, July 5, 2018. https://www.capegazette.com/article/tourist-home-milton/152818. "History of Milton." Town of Milton, Dec. 16, 2014. https://milton.delaware.gov/2014/12/16/history-of-milton/. "John Milton." Poetry Foundation, n.d. https://www.poetryfoundation.org/poets/john-milton. "National Register of Historic Places Documentation Form: Milton Historic District Amended," n.d. https://history.delaware.gov/wp-content/uploads/sites/179/2020/10/Milton-Historic-District-National-Register-Nomination_March-2020-3.pdf.

Cookin' Chicken
"End of the Delmarva Chicken Festival, Giant Frying Pan." *The Daily Times*, June 17, 2014. https://www.delmarvanow.com/story/life/food/2014/06/17/delmarva-chicken-festival/10699341/. "Giant fry Chicken Pan to Make the Rounds on Delmarva." *Delaware Business Now*, Aug. 20, 2014. https://delawarebusinessnow.com/2014/08/giant-chicken-fry-pan-make-rounds-delmarva/.

Sietsema, Robert. "The World's Largest Frying Pan—Er, Six of Them." *The Village Voice*, July 27, 2010. https://www.villagevoice.com/2010/07/27/the-worlds-largest-frying-pan-er-six-of-them/.

Freedom to Shop
On-site visit. Phone interview with Joe Capaldi, Feb. 11, 2022. Soulsman, Gary, "A Nod to Philadelphia: Independence Mall Dips into History for Design Inspiration." *The News Journal*, July, 3, 2010. "About Us." Independence Mall, n.d. https://independencemallde.com/about/.

Bees on Wheels
"Delaware Managed Pollinator Protection Plan." Delaware Department of Agriculture, n.d. https://agriculture.delaware.gov/pesticide-management/pollinator-protection-plan/. Jackson, Patrick. "Parasites Attacking Local Bee Colonies." *The News Journal*, July 21, 2002. Murray, Molly. "The Plight of the Honeybee." *The News Journal*, June 30, 1996. Tadesse, Luladey B. "Disorder Decimates State's Bees." *The News Journal*, May 4, 2007.

Only a Dog Can Hear
"Johnson Victrola Museum History." Delaware Historical and Cultural Affairs, n.d. https://history.delaware.gov/johnson-victrola-museum/history/. "Kingston's Toilet Gallery Alley Named after HMV Dog Nipper." *Surrey Comet*, Jan. 1, 2010. https://www.surreycomet.co.uk/news/4826539.kingstons-toilet-gallery-alley-named-after-hmv-dog-nipper/.

The Printed Page
On-site visit. "Books about Books: A History and Bibliography of Oak Knoll Press, 1978–2008." Oak Knoll Press, n.d. https://www.oakknoll.com/pages/books/99582/robert-d-fleck/books-about-books-a-history-and-bibliography-of-oak-knoll-press-1978-2008. Kenney, Edward L. "Publisher Is Making a Short—But Eye-Catching—Move." *The News Journal*, Aug. 27, 1998. Medoff, Theresa. "Career Happiness Grows out of Book Collection." *The News Journal*, March 13, 1997. "Oak Knoll Books." The Antiquarian Booksellers' Association of America, n.d. https://www.abaa.org/booksellers/details/oak-knoll-books. "Oak Knoll Fest XXI: Now Virtual." Oak Knoll Books, n.d. https://www.oakknoll.com/fest/. "Staff Directory." Oak Knoll Books, n.d. https://www.oakknoll.com/staff.php. Tiedge, Stacey. "Browsing for Book Bargains." *The News Journal*, June 21, 1999.

The UFO House
On-site visit. MacArthur, Ron. "2015: It's Still a Space Oddity: Hudson's Futuro House Has a Cult Following." June 23, 2015. *Cape Gazette*. https://www.capegazette.com/article/2015-its-still-space-oddity/85582. "The Futuro House." TheFuturoHouse.com, n.d. https://thefuturohouse.com/welcome.html.

Across the Bay
Bies, Jessica. "The Baja: Why a Strange Piece of Land near Pennsville Belongs to Delaware Instead of New Jersey." *The News Journal*, Sept.

16, 2021. https://www.delawareonline.com/story/news/2019/10/18/theres-chunk-delaware-over-new-jersey-heres-why/3983619002/. "Fort Mott Ferry." Delaware State Parks, n.d. https://delawarestateparks.reserveamerica.com/tourDetails.do?contractCode=DE&parkId=360113&tourId=6450&cat=1&e4q=e46bb980-dd78-4552-b581-e3815b2cef62&e4p=6e09ed89-9693-48b2-a9e5-9b940495d04a&e4ts=1646098-881&e4c=aspira&e4e=snasode01&e4rt=Safetynet&e4h=55b63b8d8d00a92f90 6f5f793c7010fa. Franklin, Chris. "A Little Piece of Delaware Is Actually Hidden in N.J. How Did That Happen?" NJ.com, Feb. 17, 2019. https://www.nj.com/news/g66l-2019/02/8d5d160f2b5307/a-little-piece-of-delaware-is-actually-hidden-in-nj-how-did-that-happen.html.

A Guiding Light
On-site visit. "Lightship OVERFALLS (LV118)." *Overfalls* Foundation, 2022. https://www.overfalls.org/index.html. Popel, Jennifer. "Dirty Hands Helped Save Floating Lighthouse Lightship Overfalls." DelmarvaNow.com, Aug. 25, 2017. https://www.delmarvanow.com/story/life/2017/08/25/lightship-overfalls-restoration-lewes/597670001/. Roth, Nick. "Weather Station, Webcam Unveiled at Lightship *Overfalls*." *The Cape Gazette*, Sept. 16, 2021. https://www.capegazette.com/article/weather-station-webcam-unveiled-lightship-overfalls/225853.

A Wedge Issue
On-site visit. Mammarella, Ken. "The Story of How Delaware Got Its Shape." *The News Journal*, July 5, 2018. https://www.delawareonline.com/story/life/2018/07/05/delaware-defined-story-how-first-state-got-its-shape/744188002/. Montgomery, Jeff. "A Historic River Dispute." *The News Journal*, Jan. 27, 2006. Shannon, Josh. "April Fools! New Castle County Tweets It's Giving the Wedge Back to Pennsylvania." *The Newark Post*, April 2, 2021. https://www.newarkpostonline.com/news/april-fools-new-castle-county-tweets-it-s-giving-the-wedge-back-to-pennsylvania/article_167d212bb-0661-51fe-8ca0-0735b5b21de0a.html. Schenck, William S. "Delaware's State Boundaries." Delaware Geological Survey, 2007. https://www.dgs.udel.edu/sites/default/files/publications/info6.pdf. "The Wedge." Delaware Public Archives, n.d. https://archives.delaware.gov/historical-markers-map/the-wedge/.

Rainbow over Rehoboth
On-site visit. "CAMP Rehoboth History." CAMP Rehoboth, n.d. https://www.camprehoboth.com/camp-rehoboth-history. Flood, Chris. "Local Author Documenting the Queer History of Rehoboth Beach. *The Cape Gazette*, Nov. 19, 2020. https://www.capegazette.com/article/local-author-documenting-queer-history-rehoboth-beach/211365. Hager, Jerry. "Rehoboth Man Beaten to Death." *The News Journal*, Dec. 19, 1981. Jacobs, Fay. "It's Officially Poodle Beach!" Letters from CAMP Rehoboth, July 16, 2021. https://www.camprehoboth.com/letters/2021/july-16-2021-cover-story-historic-poodle-beach-fay-jacobs. "History Matters: Delaware's Gay Beach." Delaware Public Media,

July 24, 2015. https://www.delawarepublic.org/culture-lifestyle-sports/2015-07-24/history-matters-delawares-gay-beach. "Rehoboth's LGBT History." CAMP Rehoboth, n.d. https://www.camprehoboth.com/rehoboths-lgbt-history.

Honoring the Fallen
On-site visit. "Copeland Sculpture Garden." Delaware Art Museum, 2022. https://delart.org/collection/copeland-sculpture-garden/. *"Crying Giant."* Delaware Art Museum, 2021. https://emuseum.delart.org/objects/10575/crying-giant. Sachs, Andrea. "In Delaware, a New Instagram-Friendly Driving Trail Spotlights Local Artists and Sites." *The Washington Post*, Nov. 6, 2020. https://www.washingtonpost.com/lifestyle/travel/delaware-discoveries-driving-instagram-trail/2020/11/06/e15f5a04-14aa-11eb-ad6f-36c93e6e94fb_story.html. "The Crying Giant." *AtlasObscura*, March 14, 2018. https://www.atlasobscura.com/places/the-crying-giant-wilmington-delaware.

Treasure Trove
On-site visit. Heydt, Bruce. "Scottish Pirate William Kidd's Last Voyage." *British Heritage and Travel*, Nov. 12, 2021. https://britishheritage.com/history/scottish-pirate-william-kidds-last-voyage. Morgan, Michael. "An Excavated Stone Fuels Rumors of Pirate Kidd's Buried Treasure near Cape Henlopen." *The Daily Times*, Oct. 31, 2021. https://www.delmarvanow.com/story/news/local/delaware/2021/10/31/stone-fuels-rumors-pirate-kidds-buried-treasure-near-cape-henlopen/8540290002/.

Hall of Famer
On-site visit. Hurlock, Al. "'Sun' Shines on Johnson Statue." *The News Journal*, April 15, 1995. "Judy Johnson." Baseball Hall of Fame, n.d. https://baseballhall.org/hall-of-famers/johnson-judy. Katzman, Izzy, and Gary Soulsman. "Hall of Famer Judy Johnson Dies." *The News Journal*, June 16, 1989.

The First Flag Unfurled
On-site visit. brown, robin. "Delaware Backstory: Famous Flag, History or Myth?" *The News Journal*, Sept. 6, 2015. https://www.delawareonline.com/story/news/local/2015/09/06/delaware-backstory-famous-flag-history-myth/71829148/. Nagengast, Larry. "Remember the Battle of Cooch's Bridge." Delaware Public Media, Oct. 29, 2021. https://www.delawarepublic.org/show/the-green/2021-10-29/remember-the-battle-of-coochs-bridge. "Where Was the American Flag First Flown in Battle? Was It Cooch's Bridge?" Delaware Public Libraries Blog, June 14, 2011. https://libraries.blogs.delaware.gov/2011/06/14/american-flag-first-flown-in-battle/.

Invention Documentation
On-site visit. Hughes, Debra. "Rothschild Patent Model Collection." Hagley Museum blog, Feb. 22, 2016. https://www.hagley.org/librarynews/museum-collection-rothschild-patent-model-collection. "Patent Models Display." Hagley Museum. https://www.hagley.org/plan-your-visit/what-to-see/exhibits/patent-models-

display. "Rothschild Patent Model Collection." AtlasObscura. https://www.atlasobscura.com/places/rothschild-patent-museum.

Nylon Capital
On-site visit. "Delaware Is Enthused over Prospect of New DuPont Textile Plant." *The Morning News*, Oct. 15, 1938. "DuPont Company Decision Hailed by Seaford Leaders." *The Journal-Every Evening*, Oct. 19, 1938. "DUPONT NYLON PLANT." Advertisement, *The News Journal*, Oct. 27, 1944. "Foundations of Polymer Science: Wallace Carothers and the Development of Nylon." American Chemical Society, n.d. https://www.acs.org/content/acs/en/education/whatischemistry/landmarks/carotherspolymers.html. "New DuPont Plant to Make Unique Fiber for Hosiery." *The News Journal*, Oct. 27, 1938. "Seaford Selected as Site for Huge $7,000,000 DuPont Co. Textile Plant." *The Journal Every Evening*, Oct. 19, 1938. Shortridge, Dan. "As Seaford Struggles, Layoffs Just Another Blow." *The News Journal*, Oct. 19, 2008. Wolfe, Audra J. "Nylon: A Revolution in Textiles." Science History Institute, Oct. 2, 2008. https://www.sciencehistory.org/distillations/nylon-a-revolution-in-textiles.

Counting the Votes
On-site visit. Cartwright, Al. "Georgetown Stages a New Kind of Return Day." *The News Journal*, Nov. 10, 1972. Frank, Bill. "Georgetown Will Rock." *The Morning News*, Nov. 3, 1976. Miller, Beth, and Kristin Harty. "Hanging from His Coach, VP-elect Flashes a Big Grin." *The News Journal*, Nov. 7, 2008. Murray, Molly. "Civility the Rule on Return Day." *The News Journal*, Nov. 4, 2010. Shortridge, Dan. "Biden's the Star, Sussex Politicos a Strong Second." *The News Journal*, Nov. 7, 2008. Stump, Brice. "Return Day a Hit for 202 years." *The Daily Times*, Nov. 6, 2014. https://www.delmarvanow.com/story/news/local/maryland/2014/11/05/behind-return-day/18568677/.

Rodney's Ride and Fall
On-site visit. Email from John Rago, deputy chief of staff, City of Wilmington, Feb. 23, 2022. Cherry, Amy. "Re-envisioned Rodney Square Gets New Fountains, Caesar Rodney Statue's Future Still Uncertain." WDEL.com, June 2, 2021. https://www.wdel.com/news/re-envisioned-rodney-square-gets-new-fountains-caesar-rodney-statues-future-still-uncertain/article_056b0f8a-c3d1-11eb-b078-c3351c94d03f.html. Cormier, Ryan. "Why Rodney Is Out and a Cartoon Horse Is In for Blue Coats." *The News Journal*, Oct. 27, 2021. Frank, Bill. "For Rodney, 'All Men Equal,' but Not Blacks." *The News Journal*, Sept. 22, 1983. Frank, William P. "Caesar Rodney, Patriot: Delaware's Hero for All Times and All Seasons." Delaware American Revolution Bicentennial Commission, 1975. https://archivesfiles.delaware.gov/ebooks/Ceasar_Rodney_Patriot.pdf. Hancock, Herald. "Blacks Played an Important Role." *The News Journal*, July 4, 1976. Kuang, Jeanne, Marina Affo, Patricia Talorico, and Ira Porter. "Wilmington Removes Caesar Rodney, Christopher Columbus Statues Friday amid Calls for Change." *The News Journal*, June 12, 2020. https://www.delawareonline.com/story/news/2020/06/12/wilmington-remove-christopher-columbus-caesar-rodney-statues/3175003001/. Schmidt, Sophia. "Enlighten Me: Statue Controversy Conversation." Delaware Public Media, Oct. 2, 2020. https://www.delawarepublic.org/culture-lifestyle-sports/2020-10-02/enlighten-me-statue-controversy-conversation.

From Sea Battles to Seafood Restaurant
On-site visit. "*Shangri-La* (CV-38)." Naval History and Heritage Command, May 19, 2020. https://www.history.navy.mil/research/histories/ship-histories/danfs/s/shangri-la.html. Talorico, Patricia. "Propelling Business." *The News Journal*, Dec. 3, 2018.

You Wanna Live Forever?
On-site visit. "Site Chosen for Restoration of Old Fountain of Youth." T*he News Journal*, Nov. 28, 1936. Cullen, Virginia. "Lewes 'Fountain of Youth' Restored, Soon to Spout Again." *The News Journal*, Sept. 28, 1951. "Lewes Fountain of Youth Restored. Open House Aug. 10." *The Cape Gazette*, Aug. 9, 2019. https://www.capegazette.com/article/lewes-fountain-youth-restored-open-house-set-aug-10/186200. "Welcome to the Maull House." Daughters of the American Revolution, Colonel David Hall Chapter, Feb. 6, 2020. https://www.davidhalldar.org/maull-house/.

Tiny Birds
"All About Piping Plovers." US Fish & Wildlife Service, n.d. https://www.fws.gov/plover/facts.html. Bennett, Chris. "Piping Plovers at the Point." Delaware State Parks Adventure Blog March 14, 2018. https://destateparks.blog/2018/03/14/piping-plovers-at-the-point/. Murray, Molly. "Plovers Have Good Nesting Season." *The News Journal*, July 29, 2006. Murray, Molly. "Early Plover Sightings Prompt Call for Volunteer to Protect Birds." *The News Journal*, April 5, 2005. Murray, Molly. "Protecting the Plover." *The News Journal*, Aug. 10, 1995. "Piping Plovers Experience Poor Nest Productivity Year in Delaware." Delaware Department of Natural Resources and Environmental Control, Oct. 21, 2021. https://news.delaware.gov/2021/10/21/piping-plovers-experience-poor-nest-productivity-year-in-delaware/. "Piping Plover Program." Delaware Department of Natural Resources and Environmental Control, n.d. https://dnrec.alpha.delaware.gov/fish-wildlife/conservation/piping-plovers/.

Corporate Capital
On-site visit. Kuang, Jeanne. "Delaware judge approves dissolving LLCs, companies tied to Paul Manafort, Rick Gates." *The News Journal*, Oct. 26, 2020. https://www.delawareonline.com/story/news/2020/10/26/delaware-dissolve-llcs-tied-former-trump-campaign-officials/6046342002/. Pileggi, Francis G.X. "Can Delaware maintain its corporate capital status." Delaware Business Times, March 5, 2015. https://delawarebusinesstimes.com/news/industry/government/delaware-corporate-capital/. Ting, Jan. "Opinion: Why do

so many corporations choose to incorporate in Delaware?" WHYY, April 27, 2011. https://whyy.org/articles/why-do-so-many-corporations-choose-to-incorporate-in-delaware/. Wayne, Leslie. "How Delaware Thrives as a Corporate Tax Haven." *The New York Times*, June 30, 2021. https://www.nytimes.com/2012/07/01/business/how-delaware-thrives-as-a-corporate-tax-haven.html

From Kahuna to Kids
On-site visit. Cormier, Ryan. "Kahunaville Closed 12 Years Ago, But There's Still One More Party." *The News Journal*, April 5, 2018. https://www.delawareonline.com/story/entertainment/2018/04/05/kahunaville-closed-12-years-ago-but-theres-still-one-more-party/489073002/. "Our Exhibits." Delaware Children's Museum, n.d. http://delawarechildrensmuseum.org/#ourexhibits. Price, Betsy. "Kidfunaville." *The News Journal*, Jan. 25, 2009. https://www.yumpu.com/en/document/read/38045751/kid-funaville-delaware-childrens-museum. Starkey, Jonathan. "Wilmington Riverfront: 18-hole mini-golf course opens." *The News Journal*, May 15, 2015. https://www.delawareonline.com/story/news/local/2015/05/15/wilmington-riverfront-hole-mini-golf-course-opens/27413281/

Laid to Rest
On-site visit. Parks, Lynne. "Honorable End for *DeBraak* Crew." *The News Journal*, May 24, 1998. Rivera, Patricia V. "200 Years Later, Services Held for the *DeBraak* Crew." *The News Journal*, May 26, 1998.

Beer Bonanza
On-site visit. "Ancient Ales." Dogfish Head Brewery, July 11, 2009. https://www.dogfish.com/blog/ancient-ales. "Midas Touch." Dogfish Head Brewery, n.d. https://www.dogfish.com/brewery/beer/midas-touch. O'Brien, Sam. "The Art of Brewing Historical Beers." *AtlasObscura*, Dec. 7, 2021. https://www.atlasobscura.com/articles/recreating-historical-beers. "Sah'tea." Dogfish Head Brewery, n.d. https://www.dogfish.com/brews-spirits/the-brews/occassional-rarities/sahtea-0.htm. "You Don't Count Carbs on a Cold, Cold Night." Dogfish Head Brewery, n.d. https://www.dogfish.com/brewery/beer/you-don%E2%80%99t-count-carbs-cold-cold-night.

Tribal Totem
On-site visit. Lambert, Sean. "Chief Little Owl: The Story of the Bethany Totem Pole." *The Coastal Point*, Nov. 29, 2018. https://www.coastalpoint.com/chief-little-owl-the-story-of-the-bethany-totem-pole/article_922591f1-b1ed-5618-b958-d03849934924.html. Talorico, Patricia. "Chief Little Owl 'Totem Pole' Keeps Watch over Bethany Beach." DelmarvaNow.com, Aug. 3, 2019. https://www.delmarvanow.com/story/news/local/delaware/2019/08/03/chief-little-owl-totem-pole-keeps-watch-over-bethany-beach/1876404001/.

Right up Your Alley
On-site visit. Mammarella, Ken. "Delaware's Ruins and Remnants." *The News Journal*, Jan. 22,

2017. "Packet Alley Featured in 'Old New Castle Day.'" *The News Journal*, May 19, 1955, page 24.

Jewish Name Game
On-site visit. Phone interview with Warren Rosenfeld, Feb. 13, 2022.

Landing Zone
On-site visit. "A Brief History of New Sweden in America." The Swedish Colonial Society, n.d. https://colonialswedes.net/History/History.html. Andrews, Evan. "America's Forgotten Swedish Colony." History.com, Aug. 22, 2018. https://www.history.com/news/americas-forgotten-swedish-colony. "Fort Christina." First State National Historic Park, National Park Service, June 23, 2021. https://www.nps.gov/frst/planyourvisit/fort-christina.htm. "Landing of the Swedes." Delaware Public Archives, n.d. https://archives.delaware.gov/delaware-historical-markers/landing-of-the-swedes/. "Timeline." Lewes Historical Society, n.d. https://www.historiclewes.org/history/timeline.html.

One Hundred, Two Hundred, Three Hundred
brown, robin. "Shedding Light on the Mystery of the History of the 'Hundred.'" *The News Journal*, June 12, 2007. "Delaware 1868 Hundreds Maps." Delaware Geological Survey, n.d. Heck, L. W., A. J. Wraight, D. J. Orth, J. R. Carter, L. G. Van Winkle, and Janet Hazen. "Delaware Place Names." US Department of the Interior, *Geological Survey Bulletin 1245*, 1966. https://pubs.usgs.gov/bul/1245/report.pdf. "How to Research the History of Your Home in New Castle County, Delaware." New Castle County Department of Land Use, 2005. https://www.newcastlede.gov/DocumentCenter/View/739/Researching-Your-Homes-History-PDF. "Roman v. Sincock." *Oyez*, n.d. https://www.oyez.org/cases/1963/307. "What Is a Hundred?" Delaware Public Archives, Feb. 26, 2010. https://archives.delaware.gov/2010/02/26/what-is-a-hundred/.

Long-Lived Trees
On-site visit, Trap Pond State Park. "Baldcypress." Delaware Forest Service, n.d. https://delawaretrees.com/bigtrees/conifers/baldcypress/. Burnett, Gilbert Thomas. "Outlines of Botany: Including a General History of the Vegetable Kingdom, in which plants are arranged according to the system of natural affinities," Vol. I, p. 504. London: John Churchill, 1835. Kennedy, Harvey E. Jr. "Baldcypress: An American wood." US Department of Agriculture Forest Service, Dec. 1972, FS-218. https://www.fpl.fs.fed.us/documnts/usda/amwood/218baldc.pdf. Lynch, Nancy. "Trees with Knees." *The News Journal*, March 19, 2014. http://php.delawareonline.com/news/assets/2014/03/WIL_0319_CYPRESS_.pdf. Murray, Molly. "Abused Wilderness: The Degradation of the Great Cypress Swamp." T*he News Journal*, May 20, 1990. Murray, Molly. "Bald Cypress Lives in Swamp, But Won't Multiply There." *The News Journal*, May 20, 1990. "Volunteers Plant 1,000 Trees in Great Cypress Swamp." *The Cape Gazette*, Dec. 5, 2021. https://www.capegazette.com/article/volunteers-plant-1000-trees-great-cypress-swamp/231444.

The Birdmen of Delaware
Bies, Jessica. "Blue Hens—the Real Thing—Will Tailgate at UD Starting Today." *The News Journal*, Aug. 31, 2007. "Blue Hen Dons Spurs." *The News Journal*, Feb. 16, 1939. "Blue Hen Now State Bird. Governor Signs 25 Bills." *The News Journal*, April 15, 1939. Kemp, Al. "Lineage Aside, They're Still Ornery Birds." *The News Journal*, Oct. 14, 2005. Nagengast, Larry. "Lawmakers Slate Official Mineral." *The Sunday News Journal*, July 21, 1985.

Meeting of Methodists
"Barratt's Chapel: 'Cradle of Methodism' to Celebrate Its Anniversary." *The Morning News*, Oct. 13, 1902. "Francis Asbury and Thomas Coke: The First Methodist Bishops Exhibit." Pitts Theology Library, Emory University, n.d. https://www.pitts.emory.edu/collections/digitalcollections/exhibits/asbury-coke.cfm. Miller, J. L. "Chapel Offers to Bury Pioneer." *The News Journal*, May 6, 2002. "The Story of Barratt's Chapel." Barratt's Chapel & Museum, n.d. https://www.barrattschapel.org/our-history.html.

Scanning the Stars
"Annie Jump Cannon Award in Astronomy." American Astronomical Society, n.d. https://aas.org/grants-and-prizes/annie-jump-cannon-award-astronomy. "Cannon, Annie Jump." Wolbach Library, Center for Astrophysics Harvard & Smithsonian., n.d. https://library.cfa.harvard.edu/phaedra/cannon. Frank, Bill. "For 'Cousin Annie,' Tribute from a College That Wouldn't Die." *The Morning News*, Dec. 13, 1963. Howell, Elizabeth. "Annie Jump Cannon: 'Computer' Who Classified the Stars." Space.com, Nov. 11, 2016. https://www.space.com/34707-annie-jump-cannon-biography.html. Jump Cannon, Annie. "Astronomy Seen as Women's Field." *The Morning News*, Dec. 14, 1931.

Feminist Fighter
"Census for 1820." The U.S. Census Bureau, 1821. https://www.census.gov/library/publications/1821/dec/1820a.html. Davis, Jennifer. "Mary Ann Shadd Cary: Trailblazer for Feminism." Library of Congress Blog, March 26, 2019. https://blogs.loc.gov/loc/2019/03/mary-ann-shadd-cary-trailblazer-for-feminism-freedom/. "March 24, 1853: Mary Ann Shadd Cary Published 'The Provincial Freeman.'" The Zinn Education Project, n.d. https://www.zinnedproject.org/news/tdih/mary-ann-shadd-cary/. "Mary Ann Shadd Cary." National Park Service, July 8, 2019. https://www.nps.gov/people/mary-ann-shadd-cary.htm. McAneny, D. J. "Downtown Wilmington Post Office Renamed for Highly Accomplished Local Freedom Activist." WDEL, Aug. 30, 2021. https://www.wdel.com/news/downtown-wilmington-post-office-renamed-for-highly-accomplished-local-freedom-activist/article_dbbb2458-09b3-11ec-8baf-731ff16bf7e2.html. Specia, Megan, "Overlooked No More: How Mary Ann Shadd Cary Shook Up the Abolitionist Movement." *The New York Times*, June 6, 2018. https://www.nytimes.com/2018/06/06/obituaries/mary-ann-shadd-cary-abolitionist-overlooked.html. "The Delaware Public Archives Unveils the Abraham Shadd Family Historical Marker." Delaware Public Archives, Feb. 4, 2022. https://news.delaware.gov/2022/02/04/the-delaware-public-archives-unveils-the-abraham-shadd-family-historical-marker/.

Every Week Is Shark Week
On-site visit. Dill, Glenn, "840-pound Mako Lands Reed in Record Book." *The News Journal*, June 25, 1989. Talorico, Patricia, "A Grand Fish Tale." *The News Journal*, May 3, 2019. Talorico, Patricia. "Driver crashes into, damages, longtime Odessa 'shark-in-a-box' landmark." *The News Journal*, Feb. 9, 2022. https://www.delawareonline.com/story/news/2022/02/09/odessa-shark-box-landmark-damaged-after-crash/6702445001/.

Skating for the (Blue) and Gold
Eisenberg, John. "Delaware Club Churns out Ice Champions." *The Baltimore Sun*, Feb. 21, 2006. https://www.baltimoresun.com/sports/bal-sp.oly.delaware21feb21-story.html. "Ice Arenas." University of Delaware, June 19, 2018. https://rec.bluehens.com/sports/2018/6/19/public-skating.aspx. Kukich, Diane. "A High-Tech Jump on the Competition." *University of Delaware Messenger*, April 2014. https://www1.udel.edu/udmessenger/vol22no1/stories/otg-skaters.html.

Carving across Delaware
On-site visit. Canavan, Kathy. "When Reptiles Ruled Delaware." *The News Journal*, Oct. 7, 2005. Kenney, Edward L. "Lecture Dives into History of C&D Canal." *The News Journal*, Nov. 7, 2001. "Michael N. Castle C&D Canal Trail." Delaware Greenways, n.d. https://delawaregreenways.org/trail/michael-n-castle-c-d-canal-trail/.

Waterproof Magic
"Creator of Gore-Tex Honored as Innovator and Entrepreneur." *UDaily*, University of Delaware, June 16, 2003. https://www1.udel.edu/PR/UDaily/2003/goreaward061603.html. Holveck, Brandon. "Secrets to Gore's Success." *The News Journal*, Dec. 11, 2019. Kay, Peter. "University of Delaware Gets Gift from Gore-Tex Co-Inventor." *Philadelphia Business Journal*, Sept. 4, 2013. https://www.bizjournals.com/philadelphia/news/2013/09/04/university-of-delaware-gets-gift-from.html. "Our History." Gore-Tex.com, n.d. https://www.gore-tex.com/technology/history. "Out of the Attic: Newark Basement to Outer Space—1958 to 2013." *The Newark Post*, Nov. 1, 2013. https://www.newarkpostonline.com/features/out-of-the-attic-newark-basement-to-outer-space-1958-to-2013/article_6f83361a8-9a63-5ff9-ad8e-aca9eb82da52.html.

Reggae Man
On-site visit. Cormier, Ryan. "Bob Marley Wrote Some of His First Songs Living in Wilmington. This Is His Delaware History." *The News Journal*, Sept. 30, 2021. Longsdorf, Amy. "Bob Marley Seen Afresh." *The News Journal*, April 22, 2012. "One Love Park." Delaware Public Archives, n.d. https://archives.delaware.gov/delaware-historical-markers/one-love-park/.

The Good Ship *Delaware*

Carper, Tom. "USS *Delaware* Will Recognize the First State's Important Role in Our Country's Military History." *Medium*, May 6, 2016. https://medium.com/@SenatorCarper/uss-delaware-will-recognize-the-first-states-important-role-in-our-country-s-military-history-e43518f0c6a8. Schwartz, Ryan. "USS *Delaware*: A Naval Lineage." Delaware State Parks Adventure Blog, April 8, 2020. https://destateparks.blog/2020/04/08/uss-delaware-a-naval-lineage/. "USS *Delaware* (Battleship # 28, later BB-28), 1910–1924." Naval History and Heritage Command, n.d. https://www.history.navy.mil/our-collections/photography/us-navy-ships/battleships/delaware-bb-28.html. "USS *Delaware* (SSN 791)." Delaware Submarine Association, n.d. https://www.ussdelaware.org/history/USS-Delaware-SSN-791.htm.

One Town, Two States

On-site visit. "A Brief History of the Town of Delmar." Town of Delmar, n.d. https://www.townofdelmar.us/history.html. "Delmar." Delaware Public Archives, April 5, 2019. https://archives.delaware.gov/town-and-city-histories/delmar/. "History." Delmar Police Department, n.d. https://www.delmarpolice.com/index.cfm?ref=41020. Shortridge, Dan. "United in 150 Years of Division." *The News Journal*, Sept. 18, 2009.

Disease Defeater

brown, robin. "Christmas Seals Were Created by a Wilmington Woman 100 Years Ago." *The News Journal*, Oct. 30, 2007. Moniz, Amanda. "Why a Social Activist Opposed Women Suffrage." O Say Can You See? blog, National Museum of American History, April 15, 2020. https://americanhistory.si.edu/blog/why-social-activist-opposed-woman-suffrage.

Pioneer Politician

Cormier, Ryan, and Esteban Parra. "Delaware's First and Only Female Governor, Ruth Ann Minner, Dies at 86." *The News Journal*, Nov. 4, 2021. https://www.delawareonline.com/story/news/2021/11/04/governor-ruth-ann-minner-delaware-dies/6285935001/. Seelye, Katharine Q. "Ruth Ann Minner, Down-to-Earth Governor of Delaware, Dies at 86." *The New York Times*, Nov. 10, 2021. https://www.nytimes.com/2021/11/10/us/ruth-ann-minner-dead.html.

Smith's Landing

On-site visit. Murray, Molly. "Long Voyage to Validation." *The News Journal*, May 30, 2007. Murray, Molly. "Nanticoke Much as Explorers Saw It." *The News Journal*, May 27, 2007. Murray, Molly. "Partnership Established to Promote Nanticoke." *The News Journal*, June 3, 2008. "Ray Mouthplates." Historic Jamestowne, n.d. https://historicjamestowne.org/collections/artifacts/ray-mouthplates/. Scott, Michael S. "A Digital Historical Geography of Vienna, Maryland: The Digitization of John Smith's 1612 Map of the Chesapeake Bay and Thomas Ennals' 1706 Map of 'Vienna Towne.'" Eastern Shore Regional GIS Cooperative, Salisbury University, Nov. 1, 2005. http://viennamd.org/johnsmith_revisited.pdf. Williams, John Page. "A Boater's Guide to the Captain John Smith Chesapeake National Historic Trail." National Park Service, n.d. https://www.findyourchesapeake.com/globalimages/user_uploads/CJS_BoatersGuide_PRINT.pdf.

Restoring Artists' Visions

"Art Conservation and Protecting Historic Interiors." Department of Art Conservation, University of Delaware, n.d. https://www.artcons.udel.edu/news/Pages/Art-conservation-and-protecting-historic-interiors.aspx. "Art Conservation: Facilities." University of Delaware, n.d. https://www.artcons.udel.edu/about-us/facilities. "Conservation Department Tours." Department of Art Conservation, University of Delaware, n.d. https://www.artcons.udel.edu/outreach/public-outreach/department-tours. Cruttenden, Riley. "Student Blog: Winterthur Museum, Garden, and Library." Department of Art Conservation, University of Delaware. https://www.artcons.udel.edu/news/Pages/Student-Blog-Winterthur-Museum,-Garden,-and-Library.aspx. Humphrey, Elizabeth S. "Preservation and Partnership: Art Conservation Course Treats Tuskegee Photographs." Department of Art Conservation, University of Delaware, n.d. https://www.artcons.udel.edu/news/Pages/Preservation-and-Partnership-Art-conservation-course-treats-Tuskegee-photographs.aspx. Malcolm, Wade. "Priceless Help for Laypersons." *The News Journal*, Sept. 11, 2012. Price, Betsy. "Del. Scientist Helps Find Picasso Image." *The News Journal*, June 18, 2014.

INDEX